Isaac and Schloyme Szwarc

THE LOVE AND LOSS OF TWO FATHERS

Looking Back

By DR. ALAN SWARC

Published by New Generation Publishing in 2020

ISBN
        Paperback: 978-1-80031-641-6

www.newgeneration-publishing.com

New Generation Publishing

To my loving mother, who was always there for me.

Alan

CONTENTS

LIST OF PLATES

1

PART 4

APPENDICES

PREFACE

The memory of my father's life did not become a significant factor in my own life until nearly 50 years after his untimely death at the age of 33. He was just one of thousands of foreign Jews, out of a total of 92,000 soldiers, who died in the Battle of France in 1940. Like them, he was registered as "MORT POUR LA FRANCE", the only tribute the Republic could offer its fallen.

For those intervening years, I felt no particular emotional attachment to Isaac (aka: Jacques).Indeed for four years after the war my mother hid from me the fact that the man we lived with was not my father, but his brother. The fact that they shared the same surname avoided the possibility of any embarrassing revelations on that score. Later, after that marriage broke up, my mother told me many anecdotes about my real father and their all- too- brief life together in Paris during the pre-war years. An array of photographs from those years, brought into my consciousness the father I had never known. And yet I really did not truly bond with him until much later in my adulthood when I began to pen historical resumes about him, mainly for consumption by my family , both here and in Paris

The advent of Friday 5th June 2020, the 80th anniversary of his death, prompted me to commemorate his memory by bringing together these resumes, my recollections from living four years in Paris and, archival material I had accumulated, into one comprehensive manuscript.

In the main, the results are reflected in the four parts that this book comprises.

Using poetic licence, the first part is drawn from my own imagination, fed by my mother's and my French family's memories of Isaac in pre-war years. After their marriage in 1938, my parents had only fifteen months together before he enrolled as a foreign volunteer in the French army. My opening theme, therefore, places Isaac on the Somme Front in the early days of June 1940.

The title of this part is "My father as a Jewish Volunteer"

The second part bridges the gap from the Armistice of June 1940 until March 1946, when a new life for my mother and I dawned. This part commences with the war-time experiences of those of my family who left Paris and those who, unfortunately did not.

The title of this part is "From the defeat of France to the liberation"

The third part attempts to convey my happy life with my mother and Schloyme (AKA: Serge) in Paris from 1946 to 1950

The title of this part is "Life with Papa Serge".

The fourth part does not pick up the story again until 1986, when a series of events launched me into intense research into my father's army life.

The research spanned a period of some 3 years and was intermittent, given my working and other commitments. But, nevertheless, it took on the character of a full investigation as each new piece of documentation and new contact, led me to explore further. Also, where the opportunity arose, I was able to visit a number of locations in France, and on each occasion, this invariably provided essential links in the story.

Although I touch briefly on the history of my father's regiment, the 22^e RMVE, it deserved to be more extensively covered, given the exceptional nature of its composition and its noticeably short existence. This important task was superbly fulfilled by the reports of a number of captured French army officers, encapsulated in the Journal de Marche du 22e.RMVE (War diary of the 22nd Infantry Regiment of Foreign Volunteers), deposited in the military archives of the Chateau de Vincennes.

The title of this part is "The Search"

In the Epilogue, I am given to musing about the course my own life would have taken with, or without, a father.

In the Appendices I reproduce a number of significant documents which I discovered as part of my research efforts.

This is a good place to acknowledge the intense work of my son, Joel, in preparing the many photographs for insertion into this book. A real work of art! Also many thanks to my cousin Maurice in Paris, now ninety years old, whose memory for detail has been invaluable. I am also indebted to the "Amicale" of the 22e RMVE for facilitating my work.

PART 1

MY FATHER AS A JEWISH VOLUNTEER

When Avraham Parizer finally entered the wood, sweating under the weight of two coffee churns, he was greeted with a series of derisory comments from his Section.

The Spanish insults he vaguely understood, but those in Yiddish left him in no doubt as to the anger of his comrades.

"We have to wait a half a night for our coffee, while you b.*around"

Exhausted from finding his way through the barbed wire   surrounding the woods and keeping his distance from the *" Attention Mines "* signs, he had some sympathy for his detractors. Some   of them had spent a sleepless night on sentry duty, whilst the others had tried to gain some sleep at the bottom of their two-man foxholes or "Trous- Gamelin" (named after the Commander of the French army).

The weather in these first days of June 1940 had been so hot that the Picardy fields around them were totally parched and full of cracks. It was to prove excellent terrain for the German Panzers when they finally attacked.

The woods had been occupied by part of the 9th Company of the 22e RMVE. This regiment and two others   had been formed in October 1939, out of the thousands of foreign immigrants who found themselves in

France at the outbreak of war. Many had joined voluntarily. Others, such as Austrian and German Jews and Spanish Republicans, had been offered the choice, by the authorities, of continued internment or recruitment into the French army for the duration of the war. Keen for the chance, once again, to fight fascism, the choice was not a difficult one. For the Foreign Legion Officers whose task was to train these men in the art of warfare, the problem of language was the first to overcome. The second, except in the case of the Spanish, who were relatively young and had already fought against Franco's troops, was the physical state of most of the Jewish recruits who were well into their thirties.

Isaac (aka:Jacques) Szwarc eagerly stretched out his tin cup to the corporal who was carefully rationing out the coffee by turning the tap on and off when the cup was half full. He resumed his watch through the trees towards the village of Villers-Carbonnel, about a kilometre away, then occupied by forward elements of the German army. All was quiet after the activity during the night, when the sound of lorry engines had breached the calm of the previous days. Everybody knew what this meant. The Germans were preparing for an assault on the French lines and were bringing up a number of infantry divisions. Today was June 4th. Far away to the north west, the last of the British Expeditionary Force and thousands of French soldiers had been embarked for England. The rest of the French Army now stood alone.

Isaac and his comrades around him were totally ignorant of what had been happening in other parts of France. They only had the orders which had been transmitted to them by Lieutenant Dufes, the commander of the Company. They were ordered to hold the wood, which was in the foremost frontal position, *"at all costs, without thought of retreat."* Isaac was wise enough to know what this meant. They were to be sacrificed in a determined attempt to hold the Germans back from reaching Paris, some 100 kilometres to the rear.

The particular task of the regiment was to maintain its various positions in the woods and villages strung out along the RN 17 and to block any attempt by the Germans to proceed either down the road or the fields adjoining it. For this, they were reinforced by an artillery unit but little else, except for a few heavy Saint Etienne machine guns and their own personal weapons and grenades. None of their equipment was new, for the latest issues were reserved for the regular French infantry divisions. Their "Lebel" rifles dated from the 1914-18 war, if not before, and their haversacks were attached to their bodies by string.

As the day passed, the officers made their way around the various companies to give encouragement for the battle ahead, and to reinforce the defences of the various strong points with barricades and other materials taken from the villages. The local peasants had been evacuated some days before and their houses had been occupied by the army. From the bell tower in Marchelepot, the Headquarters of the Regiment, officers observed, through binoculars, the preparations of the Germans in Villers-Carbonnel. When they saw squadrons of tanks moving in the distance they feared the worst, as they had no armoured units or aircraft to deal with them.

As there was no enemy activity that day, the soldiers in Isaac's Section were allowed to move inside the woods, as long as they did not expose themselves. The various languages intermingled and badly accented French was heard when soldiers conversed with one another. Isaac sat with Avraham Parizer, who by now had been forgiven for his tardiness in bringing the coffee that morning. In Paris they had lived within a few streets of each other but had never met. Their professions were vastly different, Isaac was a tailor, whilst Avraham ran a musical instrument shop. This had earned him a place in the regimental band when they were still under training at Le Barcares (Southern France).

"Tell me!" said Avraham in Yiddish, *"What is that photograph you keep looking at?"*

"It's my son, look! here he's just 3 months. That was in March. I have not had any post since we left Le Barcares over a month ago. I am sure my wife would have sent me another photo. It breaks my heart not to have held him at least once. But these things are "Beshert" (fated)".

"You mean you couldn't get permission to go to London to see them?

"I applied for it and was told it would come through, but then   the
"Broch" (calamity) occurred and the Germans invaded, and that was
that!"

"Be strong Isaac, we will come through this and you will see them
again".

"Efsha" (maybe), said Isaac, without too much confidence.

Isaac replaced the worn photo in his wallet which he put back in his tunic pocket. He lay back on the ground, stretched himself out and attempted to recall in his mind the various stages in his life which, by the age of thirty three, had brought him to this sunny but parched location in the heart of the Picardy countryside.

He recalled his arrival with his younger brother, Idek (aka: Judah), at the Gare Du Nord, on a cold winter's day in 1933, to be greeted by their parents and   Schloyme (aka:Serge)their older brother. The journey from Wloclawek, Poland, across Germany had been uneventful but tiring because of the long hours spent on wooden benches, in the crowded third-class compartment. There were many Poles on the train, mostly Jews, anxious to settle in France, the renowned land of Liberty, Fraternity and Equality, which, since the end of the Great War, had opened its gates to immigrants. This was no act of altruism, but a determined attempt to replenish the work force after the terrible loss of a whole generation in the war.

Although the age gap between Isaac and Idek was some seven years, they were, out of the five brothers, the closest. Above all they shared a passion for football and had been the mainstay of their Jewish football club, ("Stern") in Wloclawek. Now they prepared for a new life in Paris, working with their father in the workshop he had set up in the family flat. To that extent it was merely a continuation of their daily life in Poland, except that now they had all the excitement of a capital city. Although in a minority, the Jews' daily expectation of overt anti-Semitism was far removed.

Of the two, Idek was perhaps the more handsome. His face was more rounded than Isaac's and his lips were less pronounced, but in other features they resembled each other, almost by design. Their dark hair was swept back and their bodies were slim and short like that of athletes. They deliberately wore the same outfits when they went out: The same polo shirts, the same plus-fours, the same bespoke overcoats, scarves and hats. Although born years apart, they wanted to appear as twins. But their characters were quite different. Isaac was decisive, firm in his opinions and prepared to confront perceived injustice from whatever source it came, whilst Idek was softer, more timid and more trusting of his fellow man. It was not surprising that in their football team, Isaac was the captain and striker whilst Judah played in defence.

Their first impression of the Paris Metro with its smell of garlic and stale tobacco and the feeling of being trapped in an underground chamber, was very daunting. They were glad that, after what seemed an age, they eventually emerged into the light of day at Faubourg Saint Antoine. As they carried their cardboard suitcases along the street behind their parents, they were amazed by the amount of Yiddish they heard. They already felt at home. The occasional sound of French was completely incomprehensible to them but they were keen to master the language. At least their secondary education in the Polish Gymnasium had provided them with the necessary tools to imbibe a new language, in addition to Polish and German, with which they were already familiar. They were glad to note that their custom-made suits and hats made in the European style, did not make them feel out of place. There were advantages of being brought up in the tailoring business.

The flat was far larger than they had imagined and for once they had their own rooms. It was a far cry from the home they knew at 14 Ziganka Street where the whole family had once lived until the two elder brothers Meyer (aka: Max) and Oyzer (aka:Oscar) had married and moved away. Schloyme had already emigrated to France in 1928 after his father, Abraham, had brought him there on a reconnaissance visit. He established his own workshop and, in early 1932, married a girl from Wloclawek. This had been the signal for his parents to finally leave Poland.

Five days a week, Isaac and Idek toiled in the workshop with their father. Out of respect for their mother, who was very religious, all work ceased on Friday night and the Sabbath candles were lit. Neither the father nor any of his sons were in any way observant. Militant Zionism had displaced any affection they had had in their youth for the Torah. For the two brothers, Sunday was reserved for football matches against other workingmens' teams in the area. After the match, they all repaired to the "Stern" club house and entered into serious discussions in Yiddish about politics and Nazism in Germany. However late they returned to the flat, they had to be in the workshop at 6am the following morning.

And so, as the months passed by, they adapted to Parisian life and could soon make themselves understood in French despite their sing-song Polish accents. But at home, in view of the parents' virtual lack of any French, Yiddish was the only spoken language. Even when Schloyme and his wife Madeleine paid a visit on a Friday night, they quickly had to drop their usual French and revert, reluctantly, to Yiddish.

In 1934 a great change in the family arrangements took place with the arrival of the two elder brothers and their families. The rather overweight Meyer was the oldest, having been born in 1901. He had married Rushka in 1926. They had two children, Helene, and Maurice. The other brother, Oyzer, was born in 1903 and married Eva in 1928. They had one son, Loulou.

Before they even arrived, it had been agreed in correspondence, that financial considerations made it indispensable for the whole family to live together under one roof. As this would also include a larger workshop to accommodate all four sons and their father, a much larger flat was required. This was soon found in the Rue de Charonne, not far from the Bastille. At the *"Cite Landre"* there were five bedrooms, with the youngest children sharing their parent's room, one large workshop in the gallery, a dining-room, a bathroom, and a kitchen. The women, when they were not themselves working in the workshop, helped their mother-in-law in the kitchen and kept the flat tidy. This was a far cry from Poland, where both wives had relied on servants to do the more menial chores. The children were sent to Parisian schools and quickly surmounted the obstacle of a new language, but at home they knew they had to speak to Rachel and Abraham in Yiddish.

The workshop, in April 1934, was registered as a formal partnership between the father and only three of his sons, as Idek was still underage. The flat soon became a centre for Zionist meetings as Oyzer, the standard-bearer of the left-wing Poalei-Zion Party, argued for street protests against the British in Palestine and the Nazis in Germany. Isaac and Idek remained on the fringes as their militancy did not match that of the two older brothers. They were content to show their Zionism through the emblem of their football team, the Star of David.

These early years in Paris had been good for the family. Working together they had prospered and the time was fast approaching for the married brothers, at least, to find their own homes. But their loyalty to their father postponed any change in the family's living arrangements. The watershed came in 1936 when Abraham contracted cancer and, after a brief illness, died. In his last months he insisted that his bed had a view of the workshop, so that he felt that he was still engaged in its daily running.

After his death, the family left the Rue de Charonne and found separate accommodation but all close together near the Boulevard Voltaire, an area settled by many Polish Jews. The brothers continued to work together until war broke out in September 1939. But in the meantime the lives of Isaac and Idek were to undergo significant changes, as romance entered their lives.

One Sunday evening, some two months after Abraham's death, two young German refugees, Peretz and his older sister, Ida, were brought by a mutual friend to the Stern's Club house. Although the two spoke no Yiddish, the young Polish sportsmen knew enough German to welcome them. Idek, in particular, was immediately entranced by the beautiful and exuberant Ida, who was then just over 17 years old. She was mature for her age and Isaac was amused as she did her best to captivate Idek's attention. Before the end of the evening, Idek sought her brother's permission to see her again.

When a few days later he met her again, at the small hotel where one of the refugee organisations had arranged accommodation for her parents, he learnt that they were only in Paris for a few weeks. They were on their way to Palestine to start a new life and were awaiting their tickets for the boat from Marseilles. The days that followed, in the spring air of May, were all too short. Every evening, except Friday, Idek spent time on long walks with Ida along the Seine and the boulevards of Paris. His brothers were very indulgent and, under Isaac's persuasion, released him from the workshop early. On the last Friday before her departure for Palestine, Idek obtained his brothers' permission to invite Ida and her family to dinner. Without saying as much, the act of introducing Ida to his mother, represented to Idek the start of the betrothal process. However, as far as her parents were concerned, they confided quietly to Rachel that Ida was too young to know her own mind. She should therefore continue on to Palestine with them. If, however, after a while she still felt as she did, then love would be allowed to take its course. Much to his regret, Idek allowed himself to be convinced by his brothers that this was a sensible course of action. The pair then parted at the Gare de Lyon, promising to write to each other.

Isaac was happy for his brother but had no intention of falling into the same romantic trap with a girl from a different background, who lived in a foreign country. There were plenty of girls in the club who had made eyes at him over the years and his elder brothers were already hinting that, at the age of 29, it was time for him to find a bride amongst them. But for him, the girls at the club were more like sisters and he was not drawn to any of them. Anyway what was the rush? He was enjoying his life, he had plenty of friends and he was more than ever devoted to his mother who, by now, had been a widow for a year.

With the advent of paid holidays, after the election of the Popular Front Government under Leon Blum, the nation turned its attention to leisure activities, if only for two weeks in the year. Isaac and his friends, although mostly self-employed, jumped on the bandwagon. They planned a holiday in Blankenberg on the Belgian coast. Rumour had it that this was fast becoming an inexpensive popular resort for young Jews from France and Belgium and so, there was fun to be had. As work in the workshop fell away during August, each brother took it in turns to have a week's holiday, so that it kept running.

Purely coincidentally, three young ladies in London also planned to take their holiday in Blankenberg, as its reputation had even reached the shores of far-off England. For them it was to be their first foreign adventure and much time was spent on gathering together a summer wardrobe suitable for the continent. The small trio was made up of Freda Furst, her older cousin, Anne Furst and their close friend, Lilly Goldberg. There was much organising to do, passport applications, train tickets to

Dover, boat tickets to Ostend, reservations in a nice Jewish hotel in Blankenberg and a supply of Belgian francs to cover all their costs.

On the morning after their arrival in Blankenberg, they made their way down to the beach dressed in an assortment of summer wear and wearing the latest fashion in hats.

As they stood surveying the crowded beach there seemed virtually no place to sit. At that moment, a voice emerged from a young group of men sitting a few meters away. Someone called out: *"Sitz du!"* *("Sit here")*. The familiar Yiddish sound gave them confidence and they moved over to the group on the beach. The voice, she had heard, happened to be that of Isaac. He introduced himself and his friends and Freda reciprocated on her side. Soon they were all chatting away in Yiddish, comparing life in Paris and London. And so began Isaac's own ensnarement in the web of romance. The more he looked at Freda the greater the smile on his face and the more he chided her, the quicker her response. This was a girl with a quick sense of humour whose background mirrored his own. Her parents had come to England from Poland before the Great War and her father was a tailor, just like himself.

They saw a lot of each other in the days that followed and she did not flinch when he put his arm around her and kissed her on the cheek. She just laughed. After all, it was just a holiday romance.

The holidays came to an end and they had to part. Freda did not hold out much hope that they would meet again despite his protestations to the contrary. After his return to Paris, Isaac was determined that somehow he would get over to England. In the meantime there developed a long correspondence. Both Idek and Isaac, to their great surprise, found themselves in the same painful situation with their respective beloveds out of reach across the seas.

It was Idek who first breached the log jam when Ida signalled to him that she would accept his offer of marriage. After much correspondence, it was agreed that Ida would come over, accompanied by her mother, to marry Idek in August 1937. As to Isaac, he worked hard to save enough for a trip to England and, in early December, announced to Freda that he would come over to London for a few days in January. Marriage for the two young brothers was now definitely in the air to the great joy of their siblings and mother. As Oyzer quipped to Meyer *"di sehst mit Yiddish s'gibt kein grenze"* *("You see with Yiddish, there are no borders")*

The projected trip to London was, for Isaac, a daunting yet challenging task. Would seeing Freda again after so many months transform their affection for each other into something more lasting? Their exchange of letters written in Yiddish transliteration had certainly held that promise. Then, of course, would come his first meeting with her parents. Would they warm to him? How would they feel about their eldest daughter leaving home for good and getting married in faraway Paris?

These thoughts crossed his mind as the cross-channel ferry came within sight of the cliffs of Dover.

He had sat for most of the journey on deck wrapped in his heavy winter overcoat, his beret keeping his head warm. The strap from his camera case cut across his body. He never went anywhere without his Kodak and he was by now pretty adept at using it. Photography in the family was a general pastime. Ever since Schloyme had gone to France in the late twenties, he had sent back a series of studio photographs of himself to the family in Wloclawek. He seemed on each occasion to be wearing a different hat to reflect the fashion of the moment or more probably his vanity, for which he was well noted.

The train journey to Victoria station seemed interminable. But waiting for him at the exit to the platform was Freda. He was surprised to see that she had a plaster on her nose. Apparently, with the excitement of his arrival, she had lightly injured herself. She had wanted to look her most radiant and now her features were slightly marred. Isaac ignored her explanations and hugged her to him. Within minutes he knew that everything was fine between them. The romance of the previous summer had not been extinguished.

From Victoria Station, they took a taxi to her home at 74 Great Titchfield Street in the West End of London. On the way, Freda talked about her parents, Judith, and Sam Furst, whom, Isaac, was about to meet for the first time. She also mentioned her younger sisters and warned him that they would both fall for him, despite the fact that Annie had a long-lasting relationship with Harry and were destined to marry soon. As to Gertrude or "Trudy" as she was known, she was nearly 18 and already had a string of boyfriends. In passing, she noted that her mother kept a kosher kitchen, although she did not attend Synagogue unlike Isaac's mother. Her father, Sam, she described as a hardworking tailor who ,at the end of a week of toil, looked forward to an outing in London's East End, usually with his younger brother, Abram. Judith did not take part in these escapades and stayed at home with the girls.

As they mounted the stairs to the first floor there was a large commotion in the house. The two sisters skipped down from the second floor to be followed by the heavier tread of Sam, as he came down from the upper floor workshop.

They all gathered together in the large kitchen, calling out greetings in Yiddish and shaking Isaac's hand. Huggings and the kissings would come later, when the possibility of an engagement had been formalised, but this would depend on Sam's acceptance of Isaac as a future son-in-law.

That Friday evening they all dined in the adjacent dining room. With Sam at the head of the table. Judith had lit the Sabbath candles. All the best table wear had been laid out and everybody was smartly dressed to honour the occasion. Chicken soup was followed by a large roaster and an array of vegetables. Judith had been heavily engaged in the kitchen.

Whilst Freda was out walking with Isaac, her sisters were deciding what to wear and poured over Freda's photos from her holiday in Blankenberg. They giggled and passed unsuitable comments, as they ogled Isaac's manly body in his swimming costume.

At the end of the meal, the girls cleared away the dishes and disappeared into the kitchen, leaving Isaac and Sam to enjoy a glass of whisky, and get to know each other. As Isaac was staying a few days there was no need to rush things. To observe the proprieties, Isaac was lodged in the third-floor customer dressing room next to the workshop. He used the divan on which Sam would occasionally take a nap during his 16-hour working day.

Freda and Isaac had the weekend together before Isaac returned to Paris on the Monday. However they were seldom left alone, as Annie and Harry insisted on showing London to Isaac, despite the winter fog and the bitter wind. By Sunday night, Isaac had established a good rapport with Sam. After what was to be the last dinner with the family, Isaac began to sing them songs in Yiddish. His voice was so sweet and melodious that the girls and, even, Judith, literally swooned. But the effect on Sam was incredible. His eyes glistened with tears and he put his arm around Isaac. Freda then knew, for sure, that Isaac had been accepted into the family. Later that evening, Isaac and Sam spoke together and the engagement was then announced to everybody's joy. There was just one proviso, and that was they would need to postpone their wedding date until Annie and Harry were married later that year. Sam stated that he could not afford to pay for two weddings in the same year, so they would have to wait until the summer of 1938. However, he agreed that the wedding would take place in Paris.

On his return to Paris, Isaac could not wait to tell his family the good news. They were all overjoyed that he had finally made up his mind, particularly his mother who was anxious to see her last two boys married. But for now it was the plans for Idek and Ida's wedding in August 1937, that took centre stage.

Over the next long months, Isaac and Freda corresponded frequently in Yiddish. It was agreed that there would be plenty of opportunity before their wedding, for her first meeting with the Szwarc family. Until then, they would have to remain far apart in their own countries, always eagerly waiting for the next post.

On her arrival in Paris, in August 1938, Freda was taken aback by the heat of Paris and the number of foreign visitors to the Paris World

Exhibition then taking place. The family took to her at once and was entranced by her English accent when speaking Yiddish. With Ida who, from 1937, was already established in Paris, she quickly established a rapport. Both were entering new territory with their acceptance into the Szwarc family, and they enjoyed the mutual support. As photographs were the order of the day, the family, all smartly attired, attended on bloc, to a photographic studio to commemorate the engagement.

The wedding itself, was a very formal affair, with evening dress being de rigueur. The" Choupah (*Jewish Wedding Ceremony*)" was celebrated, just like Ida and Idek's, a year earlier, in the banqueting hall of the Salons Victor Hugo.

In September came the Munich crisis. Although the Prime Minister, Daladier, returned to Paris with acclaim, for having averted a war with Germany, the Jewish population had serious misgivings. The following April, after the Nazi take-over of Czechoslovakia, a French Government decree made possible the recruitment of foreign volunteers to the army. Now few were in doubt that a clash between France and Germany was inevitable. In May 1939, when Annette was born, her parents, Idek and Ita received their French nationality. The rest of the family remained Polish.

Freda became involved with some Jewish refugees from Germany and Austria who were attempting to obtain residence permits in France. She often visited the Prefecture with them, her British nationality, apparently opening doors that were otherwise sealed to them. In these times, the traditional French offer of asylum was suspended and refugees were hounded by the police, to ensure their papers were in order. If they were not, they soon found themselves in internment camps in southern France.

On the eve of war in September 1939, Freda was five months pregnant. A few days later after the proclamation of General Mobilisation, all the Szwarc brothers- with the exception of Idek- queued outside the Army recruitment barracks at Central de Reuilly. There, thousands of foreigners came to volunteer. Once registration was completed, Isaac received an army identification bracelet with the number 9683 and his brother Schloyme, the number 9684.

Now they had only to wait for their official call-up.

The British Embassy advised all British citizens in France to return to Great Britain, whilst transport was available. Freda initially ignored this advice but her fears for the child due in December, and with Isaac about to join the army, eventually convinced her to rejoin her parents in London. The pain of their parting at the Gare du Nord, on a cold November day, remained constantly in Isaac's memory, but he consoled himself that she was carrying their child to safety. She later wrote to him of the days she had spent at Boulogne waiting for a ship to England and how the officials at Dover had told her off for having waited so long.

When Isaac came home from work on 27 December 1939, a telegram from Freda awaited him. It announced the birth of their son Alan, on the previous day. The following day he replied:

"Mazal Tov, Mazal Tov to you my dear Freda on the birth of our son, Alan. Now we can say Freda, we have received what our hearts yearned for. Je suis plus heureux qu'un roi. I have become something of a daddy to a boy...."

The rest of the letter expressed the joy of all the family in Paris at the news.

In January 1940, Isaac and Schloyme were called up and transported to Valbonne, southern France for initial training. At the end of this exercise, official army photographs were taken of the recruits. Exceptionally, and only on this occasion, they were turned out in proper uniforms: rifles, ammunition belts and bayonets. The families, in Paris and London, were all recipients of these iconic photographs which, apparently portrayed the ease with which the two brothers had adapted to army life.

A month later they were transferred to the coast at Le Barcares near Perpignan. The barracks there, had previously been occupied by Spanish Republican soldiers who had escaped to France after the end of the 1936/39 civil war.

The whole training area was on the beach and the barracks were full of lice. Some repair work had been done before the first volunteers arrived but conditions were rudimentary and unhygienic. It took the efforts of the volunteers themselves, under the orders of former officers of the French Foreign Legion, to bring some improvements to their living conditions. The earth in the barracks was turned over and sprayed with a substance to kill off the lice. Lamp bulbs eventually appeared thanks to a series of visits by volunteers to Perpignan, who procured them by unauthorised means, from the local merchants.

The uniforms distributed to the men were second hand and did not always fit the men who, between 25 and 35 years old, had already lost the slimness of their youth. Even the boots were falling to pieces. New starched shirts could be glimpsed through the tears in the jackets and trousers. Some regular army clerks referred to the volunteers as the Salvation Army. Fortunately, the many tailors in the ranks were able to restore some dignity to the uniforms.

Rifles, however, were in abundance even if they dated back to 1914/18, but training was difficult in view of the lack of officers and sergeants.

Nevertheless, by the end of February 1940, training had been completed and the regiment received its official title of the" 22nd Infantry Regiment of Foreign Volunteers" (22e RMVR). It was commanded by

Lieutenant Colonel Villers-Moriame, a reserve officer brought back from retirement. It comprised 3,000 men of different cultures.

From time to time the volunteers were given 24 hours leave to visit Perpignan. Otherwise many days were spent on training marches with full equipment, so that, gradually, the men became fitter, more resilient, and confident in themselves. Although the soldiers tended to group themselves according to ethnicity and nationality, the common language was French. This was generally spoken very badly by the majority, to the disgust and frustration of the sergeants allocated to each Section.

One of the main pleasures for the Jewish contingent, was the ability to receive   letters and parcels from their loved ones and even to see them, if they came from Paris to stay in Perpignan.

In a letter to Freda dated 7th April 1940, Isaac expressed his elation at receiving 4 letters and a parcel in the same week. One enclosed a studio photograph of Freda with Alan (aka:Avremele) on her lap, taken at 13 weeks. As tears filled his eyes, Isaac wrote that he had difficulty focussing on the photo but his joy was immense. In his immediate circle of fellow Jews the photo was passed around from hand to hand. *"Di sehst. dus is mein fro un insere kind" ("You see, this is my wife and our child")* he said proudly in Yiddish.

A few weeks later the regiment was transported in cattle wagons towards Alsace-Lorraine and the Maginot Line, where a German offensive was expected. But the Germans entered France through the Belgian Ardennes. They overcame French resistance, and rapidly moved in great force westward and the Channel coast.

The French reaction was to pull back and move west to protect Paris, by deploying vast numbers of troops into Picardy.

By early June, Isaac's section of the 9th Company, was positioned in the woods (Bois des Aulnes) to the left of the Nationale 17 and to the right of, and below, the small hamlet of Horgny .To the immediate north, was the village of Villers-Carbonnel. Because of previous losses, the Section was reduced from 200 to about 140 men, armed with light weapons, and a few machine guns. Schloyme's section was retained further back in the village of Misery. Standing orders were to block, at whatever cost, a German advance consisting not only of infantry, but tanks, and artillery.

At about three o'clock on the morning of 5th June, Isaac was shaken out of his reverie by the sudden roar of an artillery barrage coming from behind the German front line at Villers –Carbonnel. He dropped into his trench but to no avail. The trees above burst into flames and he could hear screams from nearby soldiers who had been struck down by shell shrapnel. A blinding flash and he too knew no more. His life drained from him in an instant. The Jewish volunteer was no more.

Isaac and Freda on holiday
at Blankenberg, Belgium,
August 1936.

Isaac on cross-channel ferry
to England, January 1937.

Schloyme and Madeleine, engagement photograph, 1932.

Idek and Ida,
engagement
photograph, 1937.

Isaac and Freda engagement photograph, 1938.

Isaac and Freda's wedding photo with Szwarc and Furst families, Paris,
August 1938.

Back row, from left: Idek, Ida, Schloyme Madeleine, Harry, and Anne Kisberg
(nee Furst)

Middle row, from left: Meyer, Joseph Furst, Machla Ormut, David Ormut, Trudy
Furst, Annie Furst, Helene, Eva

Front row, from left: Rushka, Sam Furst, Judith Furst, Isaac, Freda, Rachel
Szwarc, Oyzer.

Seated at front, from left: Loulou, Germain Ormut, Maurice.

Isaac and Shloyme at an army training camp, January 1940.

First photograph of Alan (aged13 weeks) with Freda sent to Isaac at Le Barcares, April 1940

PART 2

FROM THE DEFEAT OF FRANCE TO THE LIBERATION

My mother received a telegram. It reported that my father was missing, believed killed. She understood the meaning perfectly well and took herself to her room to absorb the terrible news. The rest of the family were also distraught. But a six-month-old baby had to be attended to, so despite the intense pain, life had to go on.

Letters to the Red Cross in Geneva gave no news of my father's fate and, as the days wore on, everybody had to accept the inevitable.

Shortly after, an announcement came from the war-time cabinet that children had to be evacuated from London.

My mother and I were evacuated to Scotland during the worst part of the Blitz that followed. News came through, from Oyzer, that Schloyme was alive. On a postcard, he had informed the family that he had been taken into captivity on 6th June 1940 and was in a German POW camp. Information on the postcard was limited by space and censorship, but he imparted that Jewish prisoners were treated exactly as other French soldiers. There was no discrimination.

As the bombing of London eased up, my mother and I were permitted to return to my grandparents' house in London. My mother resumed work and was employed by the well-known studio photographer, Boris Bennett. He had started his career in the East End of London, where he was reputed to be able to remove any signs of pregnancy, from wedding photographs.

Whilst my mother was at work, my grandmother saw to my daily needs. By all accounts, I was very cherished by all the family, my grandfather in particular. He would often come down from his workshop in the hope of being allowed to pick me up, but this was strictly regulated by my grandmother, as I had to have my regular sleep.

I did not escape the bombing and was often rushed, by my grandfather, in my carrycot to a local shelter, accompanied by the rest of the household. There we all spent the night, with hundreds of others. I never did discover from my mother how she spent those long war years and how the loss of my father affected her. Did she resume some form of social life? Or was all her attention devoted to me and earning a living? Later, I remember seeing a photograph of her wearing a "Free French" insignia on her costume, the emblem of the French troops, stationed in England, under the command of General Charles de Gaulle.

I was eventually evacuated to a kindergarten in Kent with my cousin Angela, of a similar age. Here my first recollections began. I remember looking forward to my mother's visits. When the war finally ended in May 1945, I was brought home. I was then five and a half years old. The homeward train journey was an adventure and I was fascinated by the telegraph lines, which seemed to go up and down.

I know now that my mother, as soon as she could obtain the necessary documents, travelled alone to France in December 1945. There were important matters to attend to. But the first encounter with the remnants of the family, after 6 years, must have been a very emotional moment for all concerned. Meeting my paternal grandmother who had lost two sons and a daughter-in-law during the war was, perhaps, the most difficult part.

By then, my mother knew my father had been buried in the military cemetery in Villers-Carbonnel. Having only intermittent contact with the family during the war years, my mother closely questioned Oyzer and Meyer about their life during that period. According to my cousin Maurice (now 90 years old) who was present, she would have learnt the following:

With the outbreak of war in 1939, children were evacuated from Paris. Maurice and Loulou were sent south to Moissac (Tarn and Garrone) to join a colony of "Eclaireures Israelites de France" (EIF) (French Jewish Scouts). This was the youth organisation of the Consistoire Centrale in Paris, the main Jewish organisation.

Tragedy struck the family in February 1940, when Eva, Oyzer's wife died in Paris from a chronic illness. Oyzer made a hasty, but brief, visit to Moissac to impart the sad news to Loulou. He returned to Paris to await his own call-up, in the knowledge that Loulou remained in safe hands and had the companionship of his cousin, Maurice, just two years older.

Three months later it was Oyzer's and Meyer's turn to be called up. They were transported to a major army depot at Septfonds, also in the Tarn and Garonne. In view of their ages, they were integrated into the pioneer corps. To be near them, Rushka took Helene and left Paris for Moissac.

With the impending arrival of the German army in Paris after the Armistice signature of 23rd June, Idek also moved his household into the same area.

After he and Meyer were demobilised in August 1940, Oyzer moved to Annemasse, near the Swiss border, whilst Meyer returned to his immediate family in Moissac. By then France had been divided into two zones, separated by a demarcation line. The Germans occupied the north but the new Vichy Government was allowed to operate in the so-called" Free Zone", in the south.

As to Idek, he returned to Paris with his household and Loulou, against the advice of his brothers.

In early 1941, Oyzer arranged for Loulou to leave Paris and travel to Moissac to re-join Maurice in the EIF, now formally recognised by the Vichy Government.

A month later, at Oyzer's request, Loulou joined him in Annemasse.

Maurice still remembers how they both saluted the Tricolor every morning and sang a *"patriotic song"* to Marshall Phillipe Petain, the Head of Vichy. It has to be recognised that, at the time, the majority of the French population approved of Petain and his policy of collaboration with the Germans. There was no resistance to speak of, and the French Communist Party remained virtually dormant, until Hitler broke his pact with Stalin and invaded Russia in June 1941.

For the record, here is the refrain from the *"patriotic song"*

"Mareshal, Nous voila!

Devant toi, le sauveur de la France

Nous jurons, nous tes gars, de server et de suivre tes pas.

Marechal nous voila

Tu nous a redonne l'esperance

La Patrie renaitra,

Maréchal, Maréchal, nous voilà !"

*[*Translation*: "Marshall! Here we are, before you, the saviour of France. We promise, we your boys, to serve and to follow in your footsteps. Marshall here we are! You have renewed our hope. Our country will live again. Marshall, Marshall, Here we are!"]*

In November 1942, when the Germans invaded the" Free Zone", Oyzer recognised that the situation of the remaining two children in Moissac was becoming precarious. With the emergency dispersal of the EIF, Helene and Maurice were sent to him in Annemasse. Their parents took on new identities with false papers arranged by the mayor of Moissac. Within days of their arrival, Maurice and Loulou were smuggled into Switzerland by French peasants, who crossed the border every day for work. Because of their age, the Swiss authorities did not repatriate them to France. Instead, they were placed by the Red Cross with Catholic families. But when in turn, Oyzer and Helene also illegally crossed the border, they were immediately arrested. Helene, being under 16, was sent off to work as a domestic servant. Oyzer, however, was interned in a "Campo Lavoro". (Work camp in the Italian-speaking region).

In 1943, he was liberated because of ill-health and gathered the children to him. He arranged their placement in a Zionist children's centre in Versois, where they were taught Hebrew and Jewish history. The effect on the children soon manifested itself. Loulou became religious, whilst Maurice embraced Zionism. In both instances, they were thwarted in their ambitions. Oyzer, a secular Zionist, discouraged Loulou's religious leanings.. As to Maurice's parents, they refused to let him join the children from Versois when they left for Palestine in 1945. Three years later,

Maurice was to get his way but Loulou, out of respect for his father, never became observant.

In April 1945, with France liberated, Oyzer brought the children back to Paris.

Meyer and Rushka, after suffering many privations in the South, arrived soon after. As always Meyer carried his portable sewing machine and tailor's shears, their means of earning a living, wherever they were.

In September 1943, they had tried to cross into Switzerland from Annemasse, but the people-smuggler took their money and then disappeared. Bitterly disappointed, they took the train back to Grenoble, where they were in hiding. As they approached Grenoble Station, Meyer, always wary, looked out of the window. To his horror, he saw German soldiers checking identity cards on the platform. As the train slowed down, both he and Rushka, managed, with their possessions, to jump out of the train onto the opposite tracks. Luckily, they were able to skirt the station without discovery and get back to their home, somewhat traumatised.

Oyzer was able to reoccupy his first floor flat in Boulevard Voltaire straightaway. But Meyer and Rushka had to adopt legal means to retake possession of theirs, which was on the floor above. In the meantime Meyer's whole family moved in with Oyzer.

In May 1945, Oyzer, with his Zionist connections, organised the departure of Ida and Annette to Palestine. As an orphan, Annette received a British entry certificate and Ida, as a "social worker" obtained the same facility. With Idek's confirmed death, there was nothing to retain them in Paris and Ida's family were already settled in Palestine. In the same month Schloyme returned from captivity and retook possession of his empty flat in the Rue Vitruve. It could not have been an easy return for him.

[It would have been interesting to know Schloyme's feelings when, seven months later, he met my mother at the family meeting.]

My mother then moved her questions on to the tragic loss of Idek and Madeleine during the war. The basic stories were well-known by the family. However, to complete the picture, I have added material, from archive sources.

The story of Idek :

Unlike his brothers, Idek did not have to volunteer. He had obtained French Nationality for himself, his wife and child in May 1939, so he was subject to a regular call-up. It never came, so in June 1940, with the impending entry of the Germans into Paris, he had moved his family to Septfonds. .

Two months later, the Vichy Government organised a voluntary repatriation of refugees back across the demarcation line, and into occupied France.

Idek, without a single thought, took up the offer and together with his mother, Ida, Annette and Loulou returned to the flat in Paris. He believed that his year-old French nationality would protect them all. Unfortunately, this turned out to be an illusion.

A studio photograph, taken in December 1940, shows a relaxed family group, apparently unconcerned about their situation in occupied Paris.

All the while, Madeleine, Schloyme's wife, continued living and working at the Rothschild Hospital in Paris. She kept hoping for her husband's early return from Germany. Occasionally, she visited Idek's flat, bringing food and other necessities.

On 20th August 1941, in a second round-up, of Jewish men, the French police, under Gestapo orders, arrested over 4000 men, mainly in the 11th district of Paris. It was all done very calmly and, on the appointed day, Idek bid farewell to his family. In his attache-case, he just took a change of underwear and toilet articles. He then joined the line of men waiting calmly in the street for their transport.

A photo exists of German soldiers and French police officers herding men on to a Parisian bus. The men assumed that they would be taken to the same internment camps that were opened and controlled by the French police, after the first round-up in April 1941. Condition in those camps had been relatively good and wives and children could bring food etc.

Idek's French nationality did not provide him with any exemption. He had dismissed Oyzer's pleas to leave Paris after the first round-up, believing that the police were only interested in foreign Jews. But they made no distinction.

To their surprise, the men were taken to a newly built, U-shaped block of flats, at Drancy, in the outskirts of Paris. Conditions there were bad: straw mattresses laid on concrete floors, lack of food and a strict police regime. The place was surrounded by barbed wire and watch towers, but prisoners were allowed to congregate in the massive courtyard of the building. Initially, no German Gestapo agents were on the scene, but after a series of prisoner releases at the end of the year because of sickness, they became more apparent. Idek was able to get messages out to Ida, seeking fresh underwear etc. He claimed that his morale was good.

Seven months later, matters changed drastically. Some prisoners of French nationality, who had been allocated administrative duties, were ordered by the police to prepare lists of prisoners for deportation to Poland. A Group of 1112 prisoners, including Idek, with their meagre possessions, were then isolated and moved to   locked accommodation in the bloc. On 17th March 1942, these men were shipped out in third class passenger cars from the local station at Le Bourget/Drancy, under the watchful eye of French Gendarmerie and Gestapo agents.

The decisions taken at the Wannsee Conference, near Berlin in January 1942 were now being put into effect. The secret goal was the physical extermination of the Jews of Europe.

This first convoy arrived in Auschwitz on 29th March. Serge Klarsfeld's Memorial of the Deportation of the Jews of France records, that 1008 members of this convoy died between April and August 1942. The details of Idek's death were recorded in the Auschwitz register under the name of Juda Szwarc. Date of birth: 30th August 1914. Date of death: 18th June 1942. Registration number: 27848.

One of the 23 survivors from the convoy told the family that, three months after his arrival, Idek was clubbed to death by German Capos, for failing to sustain the arduous labour demanded. None of this was known to the family at the time.

After Idek's disappearance, his wife Ida and daughter Annette remained in their flat with my paternal grandmother. Thanks to Ida's ingenuity and sang-froid they all managed to survive until the Liberation of Paris in August 1944. Like all other Jews in Paris, Ida was obliged to wear the yellow Star of David on her clothing, under pain of arrest. A friend, called Brezil renting, at the time, Oyzer's flat, kept a watchful eye on all of them. As an Italian National, he was free of interference by the French or

German police. They did not know that, as a Communist, he was part of the International Brigades fighting Franco in the Spanish Civil War of 1936/39. After the defeat, he had slipped across the frontier into France. All the while his family remained in Italy. In 1945, he left Oyzer's flat in Paris, and returned to them.

The story of Madeleine:

Madeleine, believing herself typical of a Parisian girl, in looks and clothes, did not comply with the regulation to wear a Star of David on her clothes. In August 1942, it was Madeleine's fate to have her identity card checked by the police as she emerged from the Metro after work. The large "J", on her card, gave her away and she was arrested, for non-compliance with the regulations.

She was sent to Drancy. Within a month she was deported from there to Auschwitz. In Klarsfeld's "Memorial", she is listed as part of Convoy number 34 of 18th September 1942 under the name of Michala Szwarc, born on 7th June 1912 in Wloclawek, Poland. Her nationality was stated to be French. Despite this status, and her husband being a POW in Germany, she did not receive exemption from deportation. On arrival in Auschwitz, 556 prisoners out of 1003, were immediately sent to the gas chamber. In the Auschwitz Death registers, Madeleine is recorded as having died on

20th October 1942. At the end of the war there were only 38 survivors from this convoy

A postcard from Schloyme sent to Oyzer in Switzerland on 2nd November 1942 hints that he, at least, had few illusions about the fate of the two deportees. He notes that Madeleine had gone off, like Idek and that his morale, therefore, was at a low ebb.

During my mother's brief visit, Oyzer thanked her for acting as an accommodation address during the war. Her task was to pass on communications to Zionist contacts outside the UK, with information about the condition of Jews in France.

Oyzer and Meyer, then came to the basic reason for my mother's visit. It was to make arrangements for Isaac's remains to be brought from Villers-Carbonnel to the Jewish section ["le carre Juif"] of the Cemetery at Bagneux.

I know, from my mother's passport at the time, that she returned to Paris in early January 1946. She told me that, after arriving, she went by train with the brothers to Villers- Carbonnel. They were picked up at the station by a military jeep and taken to the cemetery. There my father's remains were duly dis-interred under French Army supervision. The Cross, which had borne his name for 5 years was destroyed and replaced by a bush. She later recalled, and described to me, the freezing cold weather and her vision of an unending sea of crosses in the cemetery.

On 18th January, a Jewish newspaper reported on my father's reburial in the vault of the "Zelbshilf" (self-help organisation) in the presence of a large crowd. The article detailed my father's military history and his subsequent demise at the front.

When my mother returned to London, I was not told that she had, in consultation with the family, taken a decision for us to join Schloyme in Paris.

Idek and family in occupied Paris, December 1940.

Newspaper photograph of Jewish men being transported to Drancy, August 1941

Ida outside her address, adjusting her Yellow Star, June 1942.

Madeleine in her flat, at 12 Rue
Vitruve, Paris 20e, July 1942.

Madeleine's police record card at
Drancy, prior to deportation, August
1942.

Schloyme in captivity, Hohenfels, Germany, 1943.

Oyzer, Maurice, Loulou and Helene in Switzerland, 1944.

Studio photograph of Freda prior to her visit to Paris, December 1945.

PART 3

LIFE WITH "PAPA SERGE" (Schloyme)

In May 1945, after 5 years of captivity in Germany, Schloyme restarted working as a tailor in his flat. Later, in March 1946, my mother and I travelled from London and moved in with him.

I readily believed that he was my brave father who had just come back from the war. From the beginning my mother encouraged me to call him "Papa". It all seemed so natural to be embraced by this very warm-hearted man, who obviously loved my mother. Although I missed my maternal grandparents, I was enchanted to be taken away, from my brief stay at the local primary school in London, to a new and exciting life in France.

From the beginning I only knew Schloyme as Serge. As a well assimilated French Jew, certainly more so than his brothers, I am sure that he preferred to keep his origins discreet and I suspect this suited my mother as well. In our "quartier" they were both happy to be accepted as French or English by the locals. In the event, although I could not initially converse with "Papa Serge." my mother passed on his favourable comments. He would cuddle and tickle me like I was used to my grandfather doing in London. Nothing could be better for a six-year old boy than to feel the love and protection of two parents.

Almost immediately after our arrival from London, my French family descended upon us. They were my cousins, Loulou, Maurice and Helene- ranging in age from 13 to 18- and my uncles Oyzer and Meyer and his wife Rushka. All began by first shaking me by the hand and then picking me up and covering me with kisses on both cheeks. I had not really experienced that before. Fortunately, my cousins practiced their school English on me right from the start. The adults all conversed in what I thought was French but was, in fact, Yiddish, their mother tongue.

I was not too happy when my cousins began to finger all the many toys I had brought with me. Quickly, they managed to break the bell on my red phone, my most cherished possession. Thankfully, they all departed after an hour, again going through the hand shaking and kissing process. In time, I actually joined in this basic French custom with joy.

My new bed, in the front lounge overlooking the street, was a lovely full-length divan incorporating a book- case on two sides. The spacious flat, on the first floor, faced a large primary school opposite. There was also a separate toilet and a small kitchen with one sink, where we all did our ablutions. Other rooms included a tailor's workshop and my parent's bedroom backing on to a very large courtyard. This, in turn, led to more modest rear flats and ground floor artisans' workshops.

Serge's workshop manufactured womens' coats for the wholesale trade. His day workers, two seamstresses known as Mademoiselle Raymonde and Madame Mauricette sat at wooden tables and sang old French songs. Serge worked the sewing and pressing machines. At night he would also work. In season, there were never enough hours during the week. But Saturday nights and Sundays were devoted to family outings and social events, of which there were many. The Metro was the principal form of transport but I also enjoyed riding precariously on the back of Parisian buses with a few others holding on for dear life. A thick chain at the rear, controlled by the conductor, provided the only obstacle to falling out.

I was swiftly enrolled in the boys-only *"Ecole Primaire et Communale"* across the street, not knowing a word of French. Among the children I was something of a novelty, I was so quiet and shy. All the children were from poor families, workers, and artisans, which reflected the nature of the population of the "quartier" where we lived. The only vehicles that stopped were motorised or horse-drawn delivery vans. In summer, the daily arrival of the ice van, with its large cut blocks of ice, was a social occasion, as housewives queued with their large basins.

School attendance was Monday to Wednesday and Friday and Saturday. On Friday nights we all went to the showers in the basement, my only proper wash in the week. The water from the overhead system was strictly controlled by a teacher. No more than two rapid bursts of tepid water before and after soaping. For me, it was all too short, as I had never experienced a shower before.

I was allowed on Sundays and Thursdays to ride my three-wheeler on the pavement under my parents' or the Concierge's supervision. Madame Graff was a strict lady with loads of hair on her face but a soft spot for me. No-one entered through the *Porte-Cochere* (former carriage entrance) of the building without passing her lodge. She had a daughter, Violette, some 4 years older than me, who also took to me. Much later, we used to go the café on the corner, across the street, to play cards. Being very precocious, she told me naughty things, some of which I did not understand but, looking-back, it had obviously to do with sex.

Suddenly, after 3 months, and to my parents' joy, I was speaking French, heavily saturated with the popular "argot" of the day. Only to my mother did I continue to speak, in increasingly worse, English. One day at school, I was taken by my teacher to a senior class to read to the boys in my *"native tongue"*. I was terribly embarrassed as I had not learnt to read before we left London. That surprised them, and all the boys laughed as I was escorted back to my class by a red-faced teacher. Well, I did tell her in advance!

Every morning, as soon as we entered class, we had to take polish from the inside of our desks, to apply to the desktops. This covered up some of the deliberate scratches, which invariably appeared. To keep our clothes tidy in school, we had to wear a short blue *"tablier"*, like manual workers.

We used dip-pens for all our written work and practiced writing in straight lines across the page until the teacher was satisfied with our progress. Mine was not too good, and the teacher recommended additional lessons. Luckily, a lady on the third floor of our building, who worked in publishing, was happy to take me on and I improved considerably.

My worst bugbear, however, was writing small compositions on a given subject and, here again, the lady on the third floor came to my rescue. On one occasion, she suggested she would write the composition and I would copy it in my own handwriting. This seemed a good idea to me so we proceeded. Unfortunately, when I handed in my supposed work to my teacher, she saw through the masquerade immediately and wrote to my parents. It appears that the lady on the third floor, not taking my age or ability into account, wrote a beautiful composition in her best literary French. To be caught out like that taught me lesson I shall never forget: Do not ever pass on someone else's work as your own!

School detentions were a-plenty and were carried out during recreation time in the morning and afternoon breaks. We had to walk continuously around two trees, four metres apart, in the school yard with our hands behind our backs, and no talking. During all of the allotted twenty minutes, the other pupils were running around us having a whale of a time.

One particular incident I will always remember:

In my second year at school, as our teacher covered French history we, inevitably, came to the story of Joan of Arc. As it progressed, I was aware that the other pupils were beginning to stare at me. When the teacher accused the English of burning her at the stake there was an outcry, which the teacher hurriedly supressed. The lesson over, we left for our break in the courtyard. There I was grabbed by some of my fellow pupils who shouted at *me "Tu a tuer Jeanne d'Arc !" ("You killed Joan of Arc.!")* I was then pummelled and kicked until a teacher intervened. I returned home in a state of shock and told my mother what had happened. She was angry and went to see the headmaster the next day. Our teacher raised the subject in class and made the guilty pupils apologise to me. She said that, of course, I was not personally responsible for what had happened to Jeanne d'Arc. They should also remember that, more recently, the English had helped to liberate France from the Nazis. Friendships were soon restored and I become something of a hero.

On either side of the entrance to our building were an array of small shops with on the right, the milk shop, the baker, the haberdashers and on the left the ladies hairdresser and the wine shop at the corner. All the shopkeepers knew me because of my mother's English accent. They referred to her as *"L'Anglaise"* a rarity in the *"quartier"*. This enhanced the prestige afforded to my father and some of it, no doubt, rubbed off on me.

The smell of stale and cheap wine permeated from the corner shop. Patrons took their empty bottles to the owner who filled them up straight from a barrel, down a long metal tube. I often peeped in but was not allowed to enter, as many of the workmen, who went for their daily ration, were smelly and loud-mouthed.

The coiffeur, on the other hand, who was next door, exuded beautiful perfume smells. His windows were full of photographs of American starlets showing the latest Holy-wood hair styles. My mother had gone partially blond before our arrival in Paris and a coiffeuse helped her maintain her Rita Heyworth hair style. The young lady who attended my mother often came up to the flat to use our modern toilet. At the time, the majority of French toilets could only be used in the crouching position, not a very dignified position for anybody.

Both bread and milk, in the post-war austerity years, were rationed. Once I had mastered enough French, it was my task to join the queues and collect our daily allocation. At first, there was invariably a young army conscript standing guard. For me, this was quite exciting, but nothing untoward ever happened. The housewives, however, in the absence of their husbands, attempted to draw the soldier's gaze to their bare legs. Skirts were worn short in those days.

The owner of the haberdashery was happy to have Serge as his customer, providing him with cottons and other needs for the workshop. In fact the owner and his wife became so friendly that they agreed, on one occasion, to take me to their parent's farm in the countryside during school holidays.

This was not a good experience for me as I had never come across peasants in the past. Dirt and poverty were manifest, even if the food was wholesome and plentiful. The outside toilet was a revelation to me and it stank mightily. I was given charge of the couple's young baby whose nappy, as the parents worked on the farm, was seldom changed during the day. I was told to follow the baby around, with its droopy nappy, as it chased the chickens. Otherwise, the couple and their parents were nice to me, even providing me with a new straw mattress to sleep on the floor. Water was pumped up from the well and the washing facilities were very primitive. This was also the first time that I tasted wine, watered down for my benefit.

At the end of a few of weeks, I was happy to return to Paris and comparative luxury. When I told my mother of the conditions at the farm she said, *"never again!"*.

I think I only went twice on holiday with my parents. The first time, to the mountains where Serge had rented a cheap shack for the three of us. A massive thunderstorm one night was too much for the roof and my mother sheltered me from the rain pouring in. This was to be the last of cheap holidays. The next time, we spent a couple of weeks in Erquy, Brittany, which I and my mother loved. It was a small fishing village with its own train station. A photo of me on the quayside showed a sun-tanned scrawny kid, whose overlong English shorts were held up by braces. I had had a good time there, scrambling over the disused tracks and climbing into cattle wagons with other boys. But soon we had to leave, as Serge was anxious to get back to his workshop, before the winter season for coats began.

The most memorable holiday, I vividly remember, was the month I spent at *a Colony de Vacance* (residential camp) organised for Jewish girls and boys, in the mountains of the Jura. An initial medical inspection was carried out at 14, rue du Paradis in Paris. It was only later that I learnt that this was the war-time secret headquarters of the *MOI ("Main d'Oeuvre Immigres")*, a clandestine Communist organisation. After the entry of Russia into the war, the MOI was much involved in sabotage operations and assassinations of German officers. Most of their leadership survived the war and their new task was to indoctrinate communist principles into the Jewish youth of France.

The camp was marvellously organised with the children divided into named groups, each with its own youth leader. There were many singsongs around nightly campfires. There were also serious lectures by the senior leadership with emphasis on the class struggle and the need for strikes against the capitalist system. This all passed over my head. I was more interested in the young girl who tended to our medical needs. She was beautiful and kind. On one particular occasion, she cleaned me up after I ate too many blackberries from the bushes, with its inevitable consequences.

Wide-games in the woods were a permanent feature of life at the camp and I learnt the rudiments of scouting, stealth and capturing prisoners from the opposing side.

Letters home were strongly encouraged but censorship was applied to any comments which could be considered as criticising the leadership. On one occasion I was told to rewrite a letter to my mother which spoke of me having been sick.

On disembarking from the return train to Paris, my mother was appalled at the state of my new, but clearly, impractical, shoes for the mountains of the Jura. The effort had been too great for the leather and all the heels had disintegrated. But, I had had a great time in the company of so many boys and girls.

My life in Paris continued to be a great adventure. My parents used to take me along to many Jewish balls that were taking place in those days. These were for the benefit of those few Jews, mainly Polish, who had managed to survive the concentration camps. Serge explained that they were now destitute, because their possessions and flats had been sequestrated by the Nazi occupiers and collaborators after they had been rounded -up and deported.

It is in this context that one has to understand the renewal of Jewish life in Paris in the immediate post-war period. Foreign Jews in, French army formations, had to struggle to gain the French nationality, they had been promised by the authorities, on their return from captivity. Sequestered property had to be legally recovered by the original Jewish tenants and vocations, particularly in the garment trade, re-energised.

About two thousand Jewish children had to be found in locations where their parents or clandestine Jewish organisations had hidden them during the occupation. Peasant farms and Catholic and Protestant institutions had to be visited by parents or, if they had not survived, by members of the "Consistoire Centrale", the major Jewish body in France, who roamed the country-side. Fortunately lists of children and locations had been smuggled into Switzerland by the rescue organisations, of which there were many. Recovery was often a delicate task where very young children had forgotten their parents and had established strong bonds with the host families.

Here, I can cite an example from personal knowledge. This, then, is the story of Germain Ormut , a Polish cousin of my mother:

As a relative of the family, he often came to our flat in the Rue Vitruve. He was born in 1931 and was therefore 15 years old when I first met him. I knew then nothing about his past. He appears in my parents' wedding photograph in 1938 with his parents. His mother Machla, was the half-sister of my maternal grandmother.

Many years later, my mother related to me Germain's sad story:

His father, David, had been arrested in the police round-up of April 1941. Klarsfeld's Memorial shows that he was deported in convoy number 5 from Beaune- la-Rolande on 28th June 1942, arriving in Auschwitz two days later. Of the 1038 deportees, there were 35 survivors at the end of the war.

On 16th July 1942, despite advance warnings from friendly police, the largest round-up of Jews took place in Paris. Machla, luckily alone at the time in her flat, was one of the 12,884 Jews arrested on that and the next day. After a few days of terrible sanitary conditions in the *Velodrome D'Hiver* sports centre, she was sent to Drancy.

On the day of her arrest, Germain, then aged 11years old, was at school. Two single sisters, friends of the parents, awaited his return anxiously.

As soon as he appeared, they pulled him into their own flat and explained the situation. The hope was that, at least, the women and children would be released. It was unthinkable to suppose otherwise. In previous roundups, only Jewish men had been arrested.

The days passed without news. Now we know why:

Klarsfeld's Memorial shows that Machla was deported to Auschwitz in convoy number 11 on 27th July 1942, just some 11 days after her arrest.

She is recorded, in the Auschwitz registers, as having died on 24th September 1942. At the end of the war, out of 990 deportees, there were only 11 survivors.

When my mother reached Paris in March 1946, she had been given a mission, by my maternal grandmother, to find Germain and encourage him to join his married aunt, Machla's sister, in the USA. She was keen, after his experiences, to provide him with a new home and a more certain future. My mother's pleadings fell on deaf ears. Germain was now extremely attached to the two sisters who, at the risk of their own lives, had saved him from deportation.

Germain, whom I contacted out of the blue in 2006, was married and retired. Initially our correspondence was warm and bore some hope of a reunion. However, in a subsequent telephone conversation, he voiced his detestation of my maternal grandmother, Machla's half-sister. He told me that his determination to stay in France was reinforced by her absolute refusal to meet the two sisters, who had protected him throughout the war years. After that outburst, our correspondence, regretfully, petered out.

From the beginning of 1947, Zionist leaders in France turned their attention to freeing Palestine, where British colonial rule was under severe attack by Jewish clandestine organisations. Oyzer was at the forefront of this campaign, representing the left-wing Poalei Zion Party, fighting to have its voice heard amidst a host of competing voices from right and left Zionist parties.

In October 1947, Oyzer had to take time off from political activities to welcome his new son, Henri, a half-brother for Loulou. One can imagine the joy in the family at this sign of renewal. Henri was to be the first child born into in the family since the war. As the years progressed many new arrivals were to join him in expanding the family. In 1945 there were 10 members bearing the name Szwarc/Swarc. By 2020, despite subsequent deaths and marriages, there has been net increase to 17.

With the help of various Socialist Ministers in the post war coalition governments, the transport of Jews from the refugee camps in Germany to French ports on the Mediterranean was in full swing. This was organised by the *"Mossad"* a clandestine organisation, whose leadership led directly to David Ben Gurion in Palestine The French Foreign Minister, was unable to stop this traffic, despite his promises to the British Government, intent on stopping *"illegal immigration"* to Palestine, at all costs.

On 19th May 1948, my cousin Maurice celebrated his 18th birthday on board a normal passenger ship, destined for the new State of Israel. He had previously obtained military training at a secret camp in southern France. On landing, he was immediately enrolled into the *Palmach*, the elite Jewish defence force. Except for a brief visit in 1949, he did not return to France until 1953, this time with a wife. In the meantime, Loulou had joined them on kibbutz, but only for a short period as, in his own words: *"Il n'y avais rien a bouffet!"* or, to put it more politely, there was nothing to eat. As to Helene, she had grown into a beautiful girl and in November 1947, at the age of 20, she married Henri, the handsome son of parents, well-liked by the Szwarc family.

Theirs was truly a love-match as Henri, at 21, was scarcely older than Helene.

In 1945, at the age of 19, he had been called up into the French army and was posted to the military police. Many years later he confided two secrets to me.

The first, that part of his duties was to escort Senegalese soldiers to a local brothel, once a week, and ensure good order. The second secret was that he had been chosen to join a firing squad. It had been detailed to execute the former Vichy Prime Minister, Pierre Laval, found guilty of treason during the war.

The execution, in the courtyard of Fresne Prison, was carried out on 17th February 1947.

In 1947, teachers' strikes, led by the Communist Trade Union, were quite common as part of wider social unrest, energetically supressed by the Government.

I had only to glance at the school entrance, through my window, to see if the doors were open or closed during that period. If closed, I had more time in bed.

I remember one aspect of Parisian life which I looked forward to every year:

The first of May, the *"Fete du Travail"* was always a jolly occasion in the street. Everybody bought Lilly of the Valley from the kids, who had found cheap suppliers. To be a communist in those days, was nothing to hide and the seller of" *L'Humanite Dimanche"*, the main communist paper, did a roaring trade in the "quartier". Serge took me to see the main parade on the Place de la Republique. Red banners flew and the *"Internationale"* was sung as men and women marched along, sometimes with children on their shoulders. On such an occasion, there was no violence, that was reserved for major strikes.

Another *"Fete"* was on the 14th July to commemorate the fall of the *"Bastille"* prison and the start of the French Revolution. There was accordion music in the streets and much dancing. Doorways were filled by young lovers who, no doubt, got up to activities that were beyond my ken.

A truly Parisian touch were the women street singers and their accordionist, who sold sheet music to passers-by.

As there was no school on Thursdays, we often went to the local cinema on Wednesday nights. Although smoking was not allowed, this was largely ignored.

Time after time, two *"flics"* *(coppers)* at the back of the auditorium removed the guilty parties amid loud protests. For local workers and artisans like Serge, the cinema was a welcome escape from the hardships of life in the "Quartier". I do not remember any restrictions on kids seeing feature films. My lasting memory was catching sight of Martine Carol's naked bottom as she got out of the bath. This became a subject of great mirth in my class for those boys, who had been lucky enough to share my experience, on that particular night.

One aspect of my life, which I disliked intensely, was my interaction with doctors and their procedures. The prospect of a doctor's visit to our flat to apply an injection was always a nightmare. Sitting in the kitchen, watching the syringe boiling away for a few minutes, was only a taste of worse things to come. The needle itself seemed so long and I had to be held firmly by my mother, when the time came.

The second procedure, which seemed the preferred cure in France for any ailment, was the suppository, which was embarrassing in the extreme.

A major medical procedure was having my tonsils out in the doctor's surgery. The method was crude in the extreme. I was sat in what appeared to be a dentist's chair with a head restraint to stop all movement. The next thing was the sudden placing of a gas mask over my face. I was told by the doctor to breathe deeply.

The next thing I knew was lying on a leather couch in an anteroom, spewing out blood. After an hour's rest, my mother took me home in a taxi, a rare treat.

Despite the pain over the next few days, the major compensation was the massive amount of ice-cream that I was allowed to swallow.

One night, as I lay in bed still recovering, Serge put a small covered bundle on my lap. It moved and as I opened it I found a small puppy. Serge told me that it was my reward for being so brave. It was such a wonderful gift, but none of us knew how to handle a live animal. Within days however, I was walking down the street, proudly showing off my new friend, on a short lead. It had not been house trained, so there were a few mishaps in the corridor of the flat, which I had to clean up. Also, it took time for "Youki", for such was his name, to learn to do his business only in the gutter. When, every day, the street cleaner opened up the system, a rush of water soon disposed of all offending waste and rubbish from the pavement which he swept in with his massive straw broom. This was how the municipalities kept the pavements of Paris clean.

On returning from school one day, I searched for Youki. But he wasn't anywhere in the flat. Serge saw my distress and picked me up in his arms and told me softly that Youki had suddenly died. I was distraught, I had never lost someone that I loved. The real story came out much later. Apparently animals were not allowed in the flats and after a warning from the landlord, which Serge ignored, he came one day with a policeman and they removed my Youki. I eventually recovered from my sadness at losing such a precious companion, but I never had a dog again.

Interaction with rest of the Szwarc family, outside of working hours, was frequent and enjoyable and I was greatly spoilt and kidded along by my older cousins. Conversation with my paternal grandmother. was limited however, as she only spoke Yiddish, which all her children and daughters in-law, including my mother, had to abide by in her presence.

I liked her because, on those occasions when my parents dumped me on her for a night, she used to give me a plum liqueur she made herself, Sharing her large bed with its massive duvet was, nevertheless, a nightmare despite the extra room I had.

I used to hate the 30-minute walk home at night from one of these family gatherings but, sometimes, Serge relented and we hopped into a taxi for the short ride.

Speaking of taxis, I was in one with my mother on the Champs Elysees one day when a policeman blew his whistle. The driver did not or would not pull over. We were abruptly stopped by other police further along. Machine guns were pointed through the windows and I got the scare of my young life. My mother remained composed and handed her British passport to one of the officers. A miracle seemed to occur, with lots of *"Excuser-nous, Madame!"* and salutes to both of us for having been importuned in this way. The taxi driver was not so lucky and was given a really hard time for his slip-up. The Paris police were very selective in their attitudes, but, Oh! what a British passport could do in those far off days.

Another grand occasion took place in 1950, soon after my 10th birthday. It was the wedding in Paris of my English aunt Trudy to Avram , brother-in law of Oyzer. Loads of family came over from London. I remember my grandfather bringing for me a white cut-away tuxedo with pearl buttons. Trudy made me promise to keep it clean throughout the wedding and gave me some English pocket money. As I was only used to French Francs, I thought it was a real treasure! My illusion was soon shattered, when Serge gave me the equivalent in local currency.

Later that year, some 4 years after my first arrival in Paris, my world seemed to fall apart. My mother informed me that we were leaving" Papa Serge" and going back to London. The marriage, in fact only formally registered in 1948, had come to an end. It was then that my refusal to leave my father led to the biggest shock in my young life. My mother calmly told me that he was not actually my father because, Isaac, my real father, had been killed in the war. Serge was just my uncle and stepfather. For me, it was all a terrible disaster. In despair, I turned to my mother for her love and protection from the worst of it.

I later learnt that Schloyme's reckless and incessant gambling was the cause of the marriage breakdown. Looking back, I remember the incessant card games when we visited friends for dinner or lunch and the frequent visits to the PMU to place bets.

For her, the marriage break-up must have been humiliating and painful as, this was the second time in her life that she had to return, with virtually nothing, to her parents' home. But, as always, she was very resilient. Work had to be found again and I had to go to an English school. My mother re-established contact with Boris Bennett, and he employed her as a saleslady in his prestigious photographic studio in Oxford Street. She was particularly efficient, in classifying and filing hundreds of negatives, for which the studio held the copyright.

Besides the bread and butter income generated by passport-photo customers, she was encouraged to exploit the vanity of better-off customers. These might be academics, local politicians, future leaders of overseas states, starlets and even the occasional criminal. For these, my mother would ensure that they were well prepared and groomed before being passed to the in-house photographer. Well before Trump expounded *"The art of the deal"*, my mother was well trained by Boris in customer psychology. From the moment of presenting photographic proofs to the customer, my mother's real work began. A mediocre colour photograph could be turned into a work of art by one of the skilful re-touchers employed in the studio. Blemishes would disappear as well as over-extended stomachs. Of course, additional costs were involved: The size of the photograph as well as the quality of the frame were important elements. Also, with many family members to satisfy, the final results had to be printed in great quantities. Hopefully, the customer would leave, satisfied with his work of art, having spent far beyond what he had anticipated. Repeat orders for prints were a common occurrence. The 50s and 60s, before the advent of sophisticated Japanese cameras for the masses, were halcyon days for studio photography.

My mother always remained a faithful employee of Boris until her retirement many years later.

I made a brief visit to Paris with my grandmother in 1951 to see Trudy's baby, Regine. Without fair warning to me, Trudy organised that, accompanied by my grandmother, I was to meet Schloyme in a local café. As a gift, he had bought me a box camera. But I felt totally uncomfortable and at a loss when, with tears in his eyes, he asked my forgiveness for what had happened. After that meeting, I did not see Schloyme again for 12 years.

There were similarities between my arrival in Paris in 1946 and my inability to speak French, with my return to London in 1950. I was quickly enrolled into the local primary school. On the first day, the children in my class giggled when they heard my poor spoken English. Obviously, only speaking in English with my mother back in Paris, my diction had not advanced.

But at the age of 10, children pick up language quickly and this was not an impediment in my studies. Indeed in one year I had to face the 11+ exams. My chances to enter a grammar school were just marginal but, with the support of the headmaster, this obstacle was overcome. Of course, I started with one advantage in my favour: I could speak, read, and write in French. The French education system had at least provided me with that facility. My fellow pupils, at the Quintin School, resented the fact that I was always top of the class in that subject.

During summer holidays, as my mother had to continue working, I was often invited by Trudy and Avram to join them and Regine on holiday at one of France's popular sea resorts (Trouville, Arcachon or La Baule). Here again, plenty of opportunity to speak French. The only give-away that I was English were my typically long shorts. Trudy rectified that problem straight away and I came back to London, after a month, with a new wardrobe. Yes, I was really spoilt!

The next years of my life in London were taken up by my *"Bar Mitzvah,"* and "O" Level exams. In 1957 I joined a Zionist Youth Movement and this, except for my accountancy studies, kept me totally absorbed for the next 4 years. It was during that period that I first came across Dorothy Jacobs and one evening, at a party, we finished up cuddling on a well-carpeted floor. It had been a brief, but pleasurable encounter and, at that point, and for the next 4 years, no romance ensued.

After 13 years living with my mother and grandparents, I was ready to spread my wings. Once qualified as an accountant, I joined an international auditing firm. In 1963, I attained my goal and was transferred to their Paris office. This was the first time in my career that my knowledge of French was a distinct advantage. It was to remain so, for each subsequent appointment.

Despite Serge's wayward ways, he was always welcomed by the family and so, it was not all that surprising that, at a party given by Maurice and his wife, he was a guest. Conversation was somewhat stilted but my affection was rekindled by his charm and his expressions of regrets. By then, I was mature enough to deal with this.

My mother had never forgiven him for breaking up their marriage, but I was drawn to Serge by memories of him as a loving father.

In 1966 I returned to London to further my accounting career, this time in commerce. It was then that I finally got together with Dot and romance bloomed. Two years later we were married and immediately went to live in Monaco. My employer Beecham's, in need of a French-speaking accountant, appointed me Financial Director of a newly acquired cosmetics company. A new adventure, this time with my lovely Dot, had begun. It was not to be the high life, but steady hard work. Our social life revolved around the English colony and there were many opportunities for tourism in the area. Dot's French greatly improved. Eventually, she acquired an interesting job as   Secretary to the Dean of the American College of Monaco. An opportunity which, one Christmas, afforded her the chance to meet Princess Grace at the Palace. The College itself, financially supported, at times, by the Kelly brothers, did not survive. There were too few expatriate students. Thankfully, Prince Rainier himself paid off all outstanding salaries to the staff.

In April 1970, after two years and tired of my posting to Monaco, Beecham's brought me back to the London head office. At the end of the year our first son, Joel, was born. He was followed 2 years later by David. Our family was complete.

The years passed and I re-established contact again with Schloyme. I was delighted that he visited us in London in 1983 .He spent time with my and Dot's immediate family. He charmed them and they all took to him immediately. I regretted that I could not invite him to Joel's *bar mitzvah* in January 1984, but he well understood that I could not confront my mother with his presence. At a later visit in that year, he spoke movingly about the loss of his brother Isaac. He told us that his Section of the Company had been held back at Misery, away from my father's own Section in the woods. When the 22e RMVE had to surrender on the second day of the battle, he desperately searched for him   amongst the wounded and the prisoners in Misery, but to no avail. With the 800 survivors from the battle, he was marched off to captivity in Germany.

Another visit by Schloyme planned for late 1985, did not materialise because of his recurring bronchitis. Soon after reaching his 80th birthday in November, he suddenly passed away in his sleep. My cousin Loulou was surprised to find that there was no money left in his bank account. Normally, despite his gambling, he always retained enough money for the monthly rent. It was as though he had planned the time of his departure.

Out of respect for my mother, I did not attend his funeral. He was buried in Bagneux, in the same vault of the *"Zelbshilf"* as my father.

One year later, an event took place, which was to dominate the next 3 years of my life.

Alan with "concierge" of the flats, Madame Graff, Paris, March 1946.

Studio photo of Freda, Alan and "Papa Serge", Paris, 1946.

Freda, Alan and "Papa Serge" at Helene and Henri's wedding, Paris, 1947.

Helene and Henri's wedding, Paris, 1947.

School photograph of Alan, Paris, 1948.

Trudy and Avram's wedding, Paris 1950. (Note my white tuxedo)

Alan and Serge in London, April 1983

Alan and Serge in Windsor, April 1983

PART 4

THE SEARCH

"Henri is on the phone". An unexpected call from my cousin in Paris. I assumed he was going to announce one of his photographic missions to a league match and looking to stay the night with us. *"Bonjour Alan, Ca va?"*

Quickly, he related that he had just cleaned out his parent's old wardrobe. He was just about to redecorate the whole flat for the first time in 20 years and had found, in an old shoe box amongst a pile of photos, a small envelope with my father's name on it: ICCHOK SZWARC. The contents comprised a metal army bracelet and various papers. *What should I do?"* he asked, I replied: *""Post them to me"*

Within a few days they arrived: A small buff envelope, no more than three inches by four, on which a metal seal had been broken. In clear French script was written: *Szwarc Icchok. 80 866 followed by 26. 11. 41*

I knew instinctively that these were my father's last possessions, somehow recovered from his body. After a brief moment of emotion, I emptied the contents on to my desk: A metal bracelet attached to one half of a disk and, separately, the second half of the disk. Both halves of the disk were stamped in the same way, on one side: *1939 Szwarc Icchok and* on the other: *9683 Central Reuilly*

At one time, the halves had obviously been attached to one another. I learnt later that the perforation between them was to facilitate breaking the disk. In the event of death, the bracelet with half the disk was left on the body, the other half, taken away, was to be used to update military records, notification to next of kin, etc.

The particular circumstances of my father's death did not permit that process to be carried out. He was therefore initially classed in June 1940 as *"missing believed killed"*.

Two carefully folded papers contained texts written in Yiddish, one a song, the other an unfinished story about a journey in a military convoy by moonlight. There were also stubs of three UK postal orders, a parcel receipt, and a short list of personal clothing.

The acquisition of these artifacts was for me, after so many years, the closest I had ever come to my father's memory. I carefully put them away.

At the time, I remember feeling that I had to know more. *Where did he die and where was he buried? How did he die?* The next years of intermittent research were to answer these and many other questions.

A short weekend in Paris with my wife Dot, enabled me to look through my cousin's family photos and document collection. Three documents were of particular interest: The first, a death certificate, dated June 1942, from the town hall of the 11th Paris district, notifying the family of my father's death, MORT POUR FRANCE, at Villers-Carbonnel (Somme) on 6th June 1940. It also stated that he was buried there. He was recruited at the Central Reuilly and given the registration number of 9683. Further, it indicated that his regiment was the 22e RMVE. [See Appendix 5]

The second document comprised, in fact, two postcards sent by Madeleine (Schloyme's wife) to Oyzer at Annemasse. The words which followed said much for Madeleine's frustration with Meyer located in the free Zone, tempered by kindness and concern for me and my mother:

This is a translation from the postcards:

"Why, for heaven's sake, impose on poor women, who have more than their share of worries, of personal difficulties, matters which one should deal with oneself? In addition, apart from the fact that it is impossible he, [Meyer] asks me to forward to him 6000 francs of rent. He forgets that for the past two and a half years, my husband is doing gardening in Germany, and that I cannot live with my wages from the Hospital. Therefore I have no savings or money to send him. Each word on this postcard highlights all my sentiments and all my helplessness. Believe me: I would give all my furniture to live peaceably with my husband.

As to Jacques, my dear Oscar, we have unfortunately learnt yesterday, that there is no hope of seeing him again He is MORT POUR LA FRANCE. and is buried at Villers-Carbonnel (Somme). All that we know is that his body was found severely damaged.

Do what you can for Freda. It is time enough to cry for our dear brother, so good, no longer with us, because of an ideal that has perished. In our hearts he will live forever. I believe you should inform Freda and the little one. She is young and, perhaps, she will be able to rebuild her life. In any event be careful, because "Maman Szwarc" does not know. My dear Oscar you see, one has to have courage and be able to accept everything stoically. The wheel turns and one always gains one's revenge when one knows how to wait. Nevertheless, I know that no revenge will restore Alan's father to life."

[Note that Madeleine refers to the brothers by their French first names. It would not have been prudent, because of censorship, to use their Yiddish names on an open postcard, the sole means of written communication permitted.]

The third document comprised an article written in a Yiddish newspaper under an army photograph of my father. This reported the re-interment of his remains, in the presence of a large congregation, at the Paris Cemetery of Bagneux on 18th January 1946.

These documents were a start in my research, but I was determined to learn more. The next challenge was, if possible, to obtain information on his regiment, the 22e RMVE and on his own particular army service.

I explained my need to my Citroen colleagues at the Paris HQ. Luckily, one of them, still on the army reserves, had some good contacts. I was soon directed to apply to the Chateau de Vincennes, where contemporary army archives were kept. Not only that, they were available for inspection, given 24 hours- notice.

A fortuitous summons to a meeting in Paris in November 1987, enabled me to take an afternoon off and visit the Chateau. Armed with my father's death certificate, a plea for dispensation from the 24 hour-rule and, no doubt, the fact that I was British, produced an immediate permission to inspect the *"Journal de Marche de la 22e RMVE"*. In the" *Salle de Consultation"* I was told to sit and wait at one of the study desks. Around me were quite a number of military researchers of all ages (including, at least, two generals). I awaited the chronicle with some trepidation. *Would I, in fact, find any mention of my father within the regimental records?*

After a quarter of an hour, a grey cardboard box, closed with a ribbon, was deposited on my desk. The label bore the inscription that it was "Carton N0.34N319: 21e, 22e et 23e RMVE". So, in fact, there had not been just one but, seemingly, 3 foreign volunteer regiments formed in the French army.

On opening the box, I found 3 files, one for each regiment, the fattest being that of the 22e. I opted to inspect just that one and replaced the others.

I spent the next 3 hours, until closing time, feverishly reading through documents and, where possible, taking photocopies. At 1fr50 per copy, I had soon spent over £10, but each document was a revelation.

The most important find was a typewritten 41-page document *entitled "Historique du 22e RMVE"*. It comprised the history of the regiment from its creation in October 1939 to its destruction on 6th June 1940. Other documents lent support to this major piece of work which concentrated its attention on the short period of 3 days from 4th to 6th June. That is when the 22e RMVE stood and fought, against overwhelming odds, in the sector of the Somme it had been detailed to defend. The battle which, effectively, lasted 2 days, was described in great detail, hour by hour, with the support of hand-drawn maps of the area.

I particularly looked for documents pertaining to the 9th company of the 3rd battalion of the Regiment, as I knew that my father had been part of it.

I was fortunate to find a typewritten report dated May 1941, completed by a Lieutenant Dufes, commander of the 9th Company. [see Appendix 1] This covered, in some detail, the activity of this unit until 5th June 1940. What was already clear was the high casualty rate suffered in the first hours of the German artillery barrage on the wood in which the 9th Company was hidden. By 6.30 am, the remnants of the Company finally emerged and escaped to the relative safety of the second line of defence, some 2 kilometres to the rear.

I suspected then-and it was confirmed to me later by a survivor-that my father had not left the wood. The *"Historique"* confirmed that the Germans were in possession of the wood at 8.30am.

I found no reference to my father in any of the documents. Only specific officers were referred to by name, all other ranks were simply called *"La Troupe"*

When I returned to London, I spent many hours reading and analysing the few documents, I had photocopied. The overall impression was one of incredible bravery in the face of an onslaught which, given the material superiority of the German forces, in equipment and men, could not possibly have been repulsed. The 22e RMVE had no air cover or tank support. It was poorly equipped with out-of-date weapons and was both short of munitions and food. The ranks had consisted of 25% Spanish Republicans, 30% Foreign Jews and 45% other nationalities. The Officers and N.C.Os were mostly French, many from the French Foreign Legion.

A very damaging report by a French General Officer, dated 31st May 1940, spoke in very disparaging terms of the quality of individual officers. The sudden replacement of the regimental commander of the 22eRMVE, just days before the battle, suggests a knee-jerk and panic reaction.

Unsurprisingly, the reports written a few months later, by captive officers taken to Germany, gloss over this particular occurrence.

By now, I had a made a quantum leap forward. From then on I lived and breathed the 22e RMVE. To increase my knowledge, I obtained from the Imperial War Museum, material on the particular period leading to the fall of France and the Armistice of 23rd June 1940.

But documents and maps were not sufficient for my needs and an idea took hold in my mind during the winter of 1987/1988. It seemed a natural extension of my search that, when an opportunity arose, I should personally visit the battlefield where my father had died.

At the end of June 1988, I wrote to the French Ministry of Ex-Servicemen, asking in which cemetery my father had been buried. An answer was forthcoming some time later, but in the meantime I prepared my visit to Villers-Carbonnel.

I discussed the trip with my family. They gave me every encouragement and my eldest son, Joel, 17 ½ years old, volunteered to join me. This gave me immense satisfaction. For my mother, this was an important pilgrimage. I no longer felt alone with my obsession.

On Friday, 29th July, we set off in the early hours of the morning by car for Dover. By 11 o'clock, after a speedy drive through Northern France, we arrived at the outskirts of Villers-Carbonnel , a small village just south of the Somme river.

The military cemetery located on the St.Amiens – Saint Quentin road, a few yards from the village, seemed to offer the best starting point. We entered through a low gate into what was, literally, a field of crosses.

There was a monument to the war-dead and at the rear a flag pole from which flew the Tricolor. All the graves appeared to be those of the 1914/18 war, or so it seemed at first. It was only when we moved to the rear of the cemetery that we found a single row of crosses, interspersed, with flowering bushes, where lay soldiers of the 22^e RMVE. The graves were numbered consecutively, except where a bush lay between two crosses. Many crosses bore Jewish names: Rachmil Waksman, Avraham Teperman and Avraham Rosner. Others bore the names of Spanish soldiers Louis Vogin, Fanes Espasa and one simply bearing the words" *Unknown French soldier*".

We realised that the bushes had been planted where mortal remains had been removed. This had been done in my father's case, when he was reburied in a Paris cemetery in 1946. However, as I did not know then the number of my father's original plot, I could not identify which bush actually marked his former grave.

The lawns of the cemetery were beautifully maintained. In a visitor's book deposited in a gatepost, I found an English inscription which perplexed me for a while: *"46 years later, one survivor of the 22nd RMVE* *remembers and salutes his comrades. Rest in Peace. P.D. 6th March, 1986"*. Could there have been British nationals in the 22ᵉ RMVE?

We drove further along the road and immediately branched off to the right, following a sign to Horgny. This place had particular significance, as the *"Historique"* indicated that it was from here that the Germans had launched their attack on the wood occupied by the 9th company.

We came to a farm, near a duck pond and stopped the car. Leaning out of a farmhouse window, and smoking the inevitable Gauloise, was a grey-haired man wearing a cap. I went over to him and asked if we could continue on foot up the adjoining footpath. I knew, from my map, that this led across a field to the wood. Daniel nodded, and on the spur of the moment, I blurted out what we were doing there.

He did not seem surprised and explained that every year, former members of the 22ᵉ RMVE came on a pilgrimage to the villages of the area where the battle had been fought. Indeed, there were many plaques and memorials to the 22e RMVE to be found in the vicinity. He went on to say that, after the battle was over, and the Germans were in full control, the inhabitants of the villages, who had been evacuated a few miles to the rear, came back to re-occupy their houses and farms.

Our guide was a lad of twenty at the time. In his farmhouse he found signs of recent occupation by German soldiers. The piano was full of grenades and the paths were strewn with field dressings. His next comment was very illuminating: The Germans ordered the returning villagers to bury the French soldiers' bodies as and where they were found. Sometime later, the villagers erected simple wooden crosses over the individual mounds.

Daniel did not dwell too much on the details, but the work was gruesome and took many days to accomplish, such were the number of fatalities.

Our new-found friend suggested we leave the car in the farmyard, whilst we went down the steep path .This led us through a wheat field and there, on the other side, arose a large wooded area, full of very tall trees. From its position, just south-west of Villers-Carbonnel and adjacent to the National 17 road, it was clearly the *"Bois des Aulnes"*, referred to in the report of Lieutenant Dufes and therefore the wood where my father perished.

Standing in brilliant sunshine in surroundings so full of colour, it was difficult to imagine the scene of devastation which there must have been some 48 years before. Nature, with time, covers up the scars and ugly traces, leaving only one's imagination to re-create the images of war.

We walked into the woods which was on a slope, leading up to the road. It was quite dense, with a lot of bracken underfoot. The sunlight filtered through the trees and it was very peaceful.

Our progress was halted when Joel pointed to shell casings at the foot of a tree. We did not approach as we thought they might still be live. It was a bit of a shock, as we naturally assumed that the woods had been cleared at the end of the war. We guessed that rainfall had, over a period, exposed the munitions, which had remained hidden since 1940.

After a brief photographic session we returned to the farmhouse. Daniel greeted us anew and told us that he had contacted the mayor of Villers-Carbonnel, who was now expecting a visit from us.

After thanking Daniel for his help, we drove to Mr. Mantovani's farm in Villers-Carbonnel itself. We met him and his wife in the yard.

They cordially invited us into their lounge and told us all about *the "Amicale du 22e RMVE"*, whose members came every year on a pilgrimage. They showed us the *"Livre d'Or"*, a publication about the Regiment, issued by the*" Amicale"* in 1976. it was in memory of those who had fallen and a memento for their widows and children.

It was full of photographs taken in Le Barcares, where the regiment was formed in October 1939. There were also photographs of Hohenfels, Germany, where many volunteers spent five years in captivity. I quickly took details of the *"Amicale"* for future reference.

Suddenly, Mantovani produced an English visiting card. It was that of "P.D." whose message we had found in the register. His full name was

E.P.Denman and he lived in Colchester, Essex. Yet another contact to be made.

After leaving Mantovani we took a stroll around the village. We found at least two wall plaques commemorating the Regiment's brief passage in June 1940.

We found similar memorials in the neighbouring villages of Misery, Fresne-Mozancourt and Marchelepot, all locations mentioned in the *"Historique"*. It seemed as if the whole area was one vast memorial to the 22e RMVE. Almost unbelievable that the local farmers had taken to their hearts the hundreds of Spaniards, Jews, and other nationalities, who had fought so bravely on their land of Picardy, in May/June 1940.

At the end of our brief visit, I came away with one nagging question: *How and when were my father's remains removed from its burial mound adjacent to the wood and then re-interred in the military cemetery of Villers-Carbonnel?*

A partial answer awaited me a few days later. A reply to my letter to the Ministry of Ex-Servicemen, informed me that the mortal remains of my father were disinterred and reburied by the French army in grave number 999 in the cemetery on 4th June 1941. It was on this occasion that the various artifacts, including the army identification bracelet were removed from his body and later passed on to the family.

Clearly the visit to Villers-Carbonnel opened up for me a number of sources of information. I was soon to move from cold military texts to the warmer region of personal contact with survivors of the 22e RMVE.

Once home, I spoke for 45 minutes on the telephone, to P. Denman .He had been in the 10th Company and had been captured in Misery. Originally from Hungary, he sought asylum in France in 1939. He was 19 years old when he volunteered, somewhat younger than his comrades. In Germany he managed to escape from a POW camp and, after a few adventures, managed to get to North Africa and from there to England. He eventually landed up in the SOE. One comment of his was particularly interesting: He had deliberately distanced himself from other prisoners, as he feared the consequences of being identified as a Jew. He deliberately discarded his army papers and attached himself to a column of captive soldiers from a regular French regiment. He was therefore sent to a different POW camp than the survivors of the 22e RMVE, who were imprisoned in Hohenfels.

This was one of several visits to Villers-Carbonnel. I have since revisited the woods with both my sons, this time accompanied by an English local resident, called John. He owned the farm above Horgny and the Bois des Aulnes. Under his guidance, we discovered many details about the wood, particularly its use in the First World War of a concealed underground hospital. He pointed out its entrance now covered by bracken.

The wood, he said, was a dangerous place for the unwary and there were still caches of munitions, here and there.

A special occasion arose when my mother, now 78, decided to make her own pilgrimage. We were to go first to Villers-Carbonnel and then Paris to see the family and, eventually, Isaac's final resting place in Bagneux. I was delighted, but felt some trepidation, at the thought of accompanying her, on what might be quite an emotional journey. In July 1992 we set off by car for France. A few hours later at Villers-Carbonnel, I showed her the last location of Isaac's grave, where now only a bush marked the spot. Of course, she had already been there in January 1946 when his remains had been disinterred. After about an hour, she left a moving message in the register to mark her visit. Stopping further along the road, at the village itself, I pointed out, in the distance, the wood where my father had died. She grimaced and thanked me for bringing her there. We then left the fields of Picardy and drove off to Paris, just over an hour's drive away. The welcome by her 3 nephews in Paris was very warm and I know that she was incredibly pleased to see them, after so many years of estrangement. Later they drove us to the Bagneux Cemetery, to visit my father's grave. The fact that Serge's name was also clearly inscribed there, she chose to ignore. We also visited the graves of my paternal grandparents.

It had not been the emotional occasion I had feared. My mother, stoic as always, maintained her calm throughout and showed little emotion at the sites we had visited. Nevertheless, it had been a good and worthwhile visit, one she was never to make again.

On the 70th anniversary of my father's death, in June 2010, I drove with my wife to Picardy, for a further visit. In Perrone, a few kilometres from Villers-Carbonnel, we met up with my Cousin Maurice and his daughter Miriam for lunch. When later, we went to the cemetery, we were surprised and delighted to find that the crosses, which had existed for so long on the Jewish graves, had been replaced by headstones bearing the Star of David. Obviously, in the interim, the representations by the Amicale of the 22eRMVE had finally borne fruit. Our visit to the woods had to be carefully managed. The terrain for Maurice, in particular, was quite difficult for a man of 80, despite his enthusiasm not to miss out on anything. He had already carefully studied maps of the area and the *"Historique of the 22eRMVE"* so he was well acquainted with the subject matter.

Much earlier, my contact with the *"Amicale"* in Paris, had provided me with a copy of the *"Livre D'Or"*. I well remember it's arrival by post on Yom Kippur 1988.

Despite my pangs of hunger after the traditional 24-hour fast, I could hardly wait to pour over its pages. I searched for a photograph of my father or his brother Schloyme. Happily, I found both: One of my father at the camp and one of Schloyme taken during his captivity.

In an accompanying letter, the President of the *"Amicale"* suggested I place a request in the October issue of their journal, seeking anyone who might recall my father and his brother.

The *"Livre D'or"* was a gold mine of information, particularly about daily life in the camp at Le Barcares which, at one point, contained 10,000 men.

The camp, situated on the beach between the sea and the Lake of Leucate, was made up of dozens of flee-ridden barracks. They had been speedily erected in 1939 to receive the Catalonian remnants of the Spanish Republican Army. Conditions were abysmal with , initially, a total lack of sanitation and lighting.

It was at this *"sea-side resort"*, that the foreign volunteers were sent in October 1939. They replaced the Spaniards, who had been moved, with their families, to other military camps which dotted the coast of the Languedoc-Rousillion.

At the outbreak of war, the Spaniards were offered a choice of a period of interment or, like the volunteers, service in the French Army. Ultimately they were to constitute 25% of all volunteers.

The uniforms, distributed to all volunteers, were of World War I vintage, if not earlier. Boots were in short supply and were often acquired by volunteers in Perpignan, the nearest large town. The *"Bandes Molletieres"* (protective leg bandages) was still de rigueur in the French Army in 1939. They took ten minutes to put on. Fortunately, the great number of tailors set to work to improve and mend whatever uniforms were available. It was a question of *"make-do"*

The equipment which each man had to carry was a different matter: the vintage rifles lacked straps, as did the water bottles. There was a lack of ammunition pouches, haversacks, and bayonet holders. So the volunteers obtained large balls of string and set to work. A tent cloth, carried across the body, was used to hold eating utensils and the bayonet, until a better arrangement was found.

The Germans dubbed the 22e RMVE the *"Regiment de Ficelle" ("the string regiment")* and this was how Radio Stuttgart welcomed them when they first clashed with the German army near Villers-Carbonnel in May 1940.

Out of the training regiments which were initially numbered 1, 2 and 3, were created, in February 1940, the 21st and 22e RMVE. The 23rd RMVE was created in May. Each regiment consisted of 3 infantry battalions and 4 support companies. Each battalion, in turn, consisted of 4 companies of

200 men, each led by a lieutenant or captain. In all, each regiment consisted of 3,000 men.

In April, the 3 regiments were taken to the Camp de Larsac for 3 weeks of further field training.

Suddenly, on 6th May, the 22e RMVE was mobilised and transported in cattle wagons to Dannemarie (Alsace) where the initial German onslaught was expected.

However, when the German offensive was launched on 10th May, it cut through the Belgian Ardennes into a thinly defended front in France and separately invaded Belgium and Holland. This last move was designed to cut off the dug-in allied forces from their supply lines in the south. On 19th May following the fall of the Benelux countries, the Regiment was swiftly redeployed by train towards Paris. It soon had to disembark when the railway line was cut by enemy action. There followed a journey by lorry and Parisian buses towards the new front, south of the Somme, near Perrone.

The subsequent advance towards the north had to be made on foot. Between 22nd and 26th May the regiment progressed towards Villers-Carbonnel, clearing villages of light enemy forces on the way. Two attempts to capture the village itself failed with heavy casualties, particularly in the 2nd battalion.

The regiment was then given orders to dig in, opposite the village, whilst a counterattack, planned for 6th June, was being prepared.

On 28th May, the officer commanding the 19th Infantry Division, of which the 22^e RMVE formed part, issued An Order of the Day, which said:

"I reiterate the order already given. Whatever the violence of shelling or of the attacks to which the unit's infantry or artillery may be subjected, no retreat may be ordered or tolerated. All must resist in each area until the last man, ensuring maximum losses to the enemy. The outcome of the present battle [for France] depends on it.

Signed: General Toussaint"

[The reader may conclude that, if ever this was a sentence of death on the 22e RMVE, this was it.]

On 4th June 1940, the last British troops and many French troops, were evacuated from Dunkirk. On the same day, the German High Command ordered an offensive to be directed towards the Somme and Paris.

Across the whole front, at 3.45 am on the morning of 5th June, the French, already forewarned of the impending attack, were subjected to a concerted artillery barrage, to the south of Villers-Carbonnel. A mass attack by tanks and motorised infantry followed. In the area defended by the 22e RMVE, a few strong points initially held. Over the nest 2 days they were surrounded and infiltrated, one by one.

Already by 7AM on the first day, the 22e RMVE was cut off from French forces in the rear.

Whilst other regiments on the left and right flanks of the 22e RMVE put up little opposition, the will to fight of the *"Regiment de Ficelle"* remained unimpaired. They knew that they had nothing to lose but their lives. Like the Spaniards among them, they fought like demons until the ammunition ran out. At 6.30 pm on the night of 6th June all resistance crumbled.

It is worth recalling that, out of 3,000 men, only 800 were taken prisoner. Others had presumably been killed, escaped or injured, were already hospitalised in the rear.

This narrative should end with the final words written by the Commander of the 22e *RMVE in the" Historique"*:

"The short existence of the 22eRMVE thus ended on the Somme, less than 8 months after its creation.

One nevertheless had the satisfaction of seeing it prove, in these last days of combat, that it was worthy of its forebears, because the adversary had rendered homage to its accomplishments. If it had not found itself beaten by a better-equipped enemy, it would have been counted, within a short time, among the crack regiments of the Army.

Signed: Chef de Battalion Hermann, Acting Commander of the 22e RMVE.

Oflag IV D

November 1940"

[Apparently after the French surrender took place in Marchelepot, the German commander complimented Hermann, on the brilliant defence that had been put up against his forces.]

A year later, the Commander in chief of French land forces, now under Vichy control, awarded:

"A citation of the Army to the "22e Regiment de Marche de Volontaires Etrangers", detailing its accomplishments during the battle.

The regiment was awarded the CROIX DE GUERRE 1939-1945 with Palm [gold leaf].

Vichy, 2ⁿᵈ July 1941"

[See Appendix 4. No other military formation, other than the Navy cadets of Saumur, were awarded such a distinction by the French army after the initial Battle for France.]

By chance, within one month of receiving the *" L'ivre d'Or",* with its tales and photographs of Le Barcares, an opportunity came up for me to visit the very place. It was almost as if I was on a predestined course.

The reason for my trip to St.Tropez, in the South France was to attend Citroen's annual two-day conference of European Financial directors.

Once the conference ended, I swiftly drove off in my hire car in the direction of Perpignan, some 500 kilometres to the west. Even more propitious, the rainfall we had suffered continuously was suddenly transformed into brilliant October sunshine.

By mid-day I was on the outskirts of Le Barcares, having skirted around the Lake of Leucate on the left. The place had been extensively developed as a Marina and sea-side resort with many holiday flats and bungalows in the Spanish style. What had been planned in the middle 30's under the attractive title *"Cote Vermeille"* had been more than implemented in the 60's and 70's. So, *how could I possibly find any trace of the vast military camp which existed there in 1940?*

I drove through the village to the promenade on the sea-front and found a restaurant. After a while, a snack and half a litre of Rose, I asked the *"Patronne"* if she knew of the past existence of an army camp, along the beach.

She responded that I must be thinking of an area where the *"Spanish Monument"* was situated, just north of the village. After I left the restaurant and had passed the last houses of Le Barcares, I carried on down a straight road bordered by sand on one side and the Lake on the other. A large monument came within sight. It rose like 3 columns out of the beach. As I came closer, I noticed that it had its own parking area and so I pulled in. A path, a few feet wide, led towards steps which descended to a large *"parvis"* (esplanade) on which stood the monument. It was then that I noticed a large lateral block of concrete which joined the 3 columns, some 3 feet from the base. On it was an inscription, the translation of which is:

"At this place in 1939 the fierce determination of 10,000 volunteers to resist the invader, in the full knowledge they pledged their lives for France became a reality. They formed the 21st, 22nd and 23rd RMVE. This memorial has been erected in memory of their passage"

Clearly, it was not just a memorial to the Spanish but to all the nationalities who comprised the 3 regiments.

On each column, below this inscription, was sculpted a soldier representing a particular regiment. Moving round the side of the right-hand column, I noticed a further inscription:

WATKIN-Sculpteur

VAGO-Architecte

Not one piece of wood remained on the beach, as evidence of what had once been. Not even a trace of the Lido hotel, which had stood in the centre of the camp to provide officers' accommodation.

I criss-crossed the area on foot many times over the next two hours. I hoped to see some vestige of the camp, some indication that my father had once stood on the same beach, so many years ago.

Suddenly, I saw a small Fiat entering the parking lot. I was a few hundred meters away as a small, hunched, and grey-haired man, got out. He moved away to better survey the Monument. Curious, I went over to him and entered into a conversation about his interest in the Monument, known as the *" Memoriale des Trois Collones"*. He gave me a broad toothless smile and introduced himself as Etienne Vago, its actual architect!

My surprise was immense to say the least. I couldn't let this man go without further questioning. We sat in his car and he answered all my many questions. My interest grew by leaps and bounds as he related the following:

Firstly, He had come from Paris to discuss improvements to the site with the local council. Secondly, He had belonged to the 21st RMVE and thirdly, his regiment had seen action in the forest of Norval and the Ardennes Canal in mid-June 1940 just before the Armistice was signed.

At his suggestion, I booked into the small hotel where he was staying, the *" Casa Blanca"*. The owners were very friendly and, knowing my quest, they introduced me to an elderly gentleman from Paris called Bernard Feldman.

By now, I had got used to the unexpected and took in my stride the news that Feldman was the secretary of the *"Amicale"* of the 23rd RMVE.

In the space of a few hours, I had finally established contact with survivors of two of the Regiments. Coincidence or fate?

I spoke to Etienne Vago late into the night. He was now 79 years old and came originally from Hungary, in the inter-war years.

His, was a well-known family of architects. His father, Joseph Vago, had, in 1927, designed the League of Nations building in Geneva and in 1957 his cousin, Pierre Vargo, designed the underground basilica at the shrine of Lourdes.

He told me about a writer called Hans Haber (not his original name) who had written a book about the 21st RMVE called *"A thousand shall fall"*. Haber had escaped from a German POW camp and arrived in New York in December 1940. His career in the USA spanned films and TV. He died in 1984.

After these exciting meetings in Le Barcares, I returned the next day to Nice and flew home. I was to meet Vago, once more, sometime later.

After a few weeks of research I obtained an old copy of Haber's book. I quote from page 64 where Haber describes Etienne Vago:

"A little fellow, he seemed no more than 19 years old when together we left Paris for Le Barcares. Meanwhile he had become a corporal and had grown a beard to enhance his dignity. He had a noble, Christ-like head. Even under the most violent enemy fire, Vago had spent at least an hour a day tending to his beard. He had a little comb and a pocket mirror. With oriental patience, he would stroke his soft, burnished fair hair. Never had I seen him spend a free minute in any other way. Now he lay pathetically beside me .He seemed unequal to the hardships"

The next occurrence-and perhaps the climax of the whole affair-was meeting an actual survivor from the 9th Company of the 22eRMVE. This came early in December 1988. This was prompted by a letter which had arrived from Paris in response to my insertion in the October issue of the *"Amicale"*:

Paris 3rd December 1988,

Dear Mr. Swarc ,

Further to your insertion in the bulletin of the Amicale of the 22eRMVE, I am pleased to inform you that, having been, in the 9th company, I knew your father well. I was also a prisoner with your uncle for 5 years in Hohenfels.

I enclose an original photograph which was in my possession (Your father is standing at the end on the right; your uncle is standing second from the left).

I am at your service if you desire further information.

My best wishes,

Signed: Abraham Parizer".

The photograph which I later had enlarged, clearly showed my father and uncle in a group which, I assumed, was part of the 9th Company.

What should I do next? For 2 days I pondered and then, on a Saturday night, I telephoned Parizer's home. It was his son who answered and obviously aware of the letter (He had written it for his father), suggested I call back later when his father would be home. As I was going out that evening, I had to leave the call until the following night.

The voice that answered me on my second call, immediately evoked in me memories of my late uncles. The sing-song Yiddish accent of that generation came through his clearly spoken French.

We spoke for 45 minutes and it seemed like a brief moment. His memory for detail was quite incredible for a man of 79. His enthusiasm to help me fill in the blanks was very heart-warming. We agreed to meet in Paris for another, but longer discussion, when the opportunity of a business trip presented itself for me. For the first time, I was about to establish an almost tangible link with my father through the memory of one of his comrades-in-arms. I was anxious, in view of his age, to meet him soon.

On past experience, a business trip to Paris in the winter months was unlikely and I had already been there in November. Incidentally, this had provided me with a second visit to the archives in the Chateau de Vincennes, to acquire even more photocopies.

Fortune smiled on me, yet again, and I received an invitation to Citroen's Paris headquarters for the end of January 1989.

With a Tuesday meeting, I could plan to be in Paris for the previous weekend, and so spend time with Abraham .

In the meantime, my family brought me a portable cassette recorder for my 49th birthday, so that I could retain, for posterity, every word.

After a couple of phone calls, we arranged to meet at Abraham Parizer's address, just off the Boulevard Voltaire on Sunday, 29th January. It was amazing to me that, living within a few streets from where the Szwarc family had resided both before and after the war, Abraham had not met any of them, except for Schloyme.

Again, he only came across him in the street when they both did their daily walks.

At mid-day, as I approached the block of flats, I saw an elderly man standing in the doorway, looking up and down the street. I waved and mutual recognition quickly followed. He had a wrinkled face and a strong handshake. He must have been taller once but now he was stooped. His thin grey hair covered most of his head and ended in curls at the base of his neck. He was smartly dressed except for the brown sandals, which was an eccentric touch, especially in January.

From the first moment we shared something: his willingness to share his war-time experiences and my eagerness to listen.

As we went off down the road to his local restaurant, he began to relate his personal history. He had arrived in Paris at the age of 17 in 1926 from Galicia, Poland. Starting as an agricultural labourer, he progressed to carpentry and eventually to musical instrument maker. At the age of 25 he opened his own shop on the ground floor of the building where he now lived.

The outbreak of war and the harassment of the Garde Mobile on the streets, encouraged him to sign up as a volunteer. When he was eventually called to report, he locked up his flat on the 3rd floor, pulled down the metal blinds of his shop, with its valuable stock of musical instruments, and left. He initially was sent to the training camp at Valbonne near Lyon. There he spent a very cold winter, sleeping in farm barns. In January 1940 he was transferred to Le Barcares.

Once we found a suitable table in the restaurant and had taken off the chill with a Kir Royal, I switched on my recorder and we were off.

For the next one and a half hours, I listened enraptured to his experiences in the 22e RMVE. From time to time I would prompt him but his delivery did not falter. Throughout the three-course meal, he drank little wine and only finished his meal a short while after I did, despite his virtual monologue. It was all fascinating, particularly about individual members of the 9th Company.

As to my father, they had met for the first time at Le Barcares, where they shared a hut with nine other members and a host of fleas. *"Nous etions de bon copains, il etait gentil et honnete". ("We were good mates; he was nice and honest").*

He well remembered the day a letter arrived from my mother with the first photograph of me, sometime in April 1940. He described it as a moment of supreme joy for my father and it was passed from hand to hand. As Abraham commented, my father now had something to protect.

On Sundays, when leave was available, the group would go off to Perpignan to have a restaurant meal. The state of their training uniforms was such that the local military commander complained bitterly about the poor image of the French army, which this engendered amongst the locals.

Abraham was particularly happy to be in the regimental band as a drummer, as this excused him from physical training. But this virtual holiday was short lived when the regiment was embarked on trains for Alsace in May 1940.

One officer, he particularly disliked, was the Company Commander, Lieutenant Pierre Dufes. Abraham described him as an "*Antisemite de premier ordre*". "*(A first-class Antisemite")* He was constantly escorted by two Spanish brothers, as he feared for his safety at the hands of the rest of the Company

Abraham commented on the same incident referred to by lieutenant Dufes in his report of May 1941, namely the time that Dufes was struck in the eye by a branch as he was proceeding at night through the woods. Dufes indicates that after receiving medical treatment he returned to the Company. But, according to Abraham, Dufes deliberately injured himself in order to be evacuated to the rear and away from the battle zone. Abraham asserts that Dufes disappeared from that moment on. However in his own report, Dufes indicates that he only left the battlefield, when he was struck by shrapnel in his kidneys, in the early hours of 5th June It was then that he had himself transported to the first-aid station at Fresne-Mazencourt.

That the narratives are in conflict is symptomatic of the little faith that the ordinary soldier had in his officers. On the other hand, one can well imagine the distaste with which French officers of the Reserve, regarded the task of leading such a motley crew of foreigners, despite the latter's volunteer status.

Inevitably, we came to the point where I questioned Abraham about the circumstances of my father's death in the Bois des Aulnes. According to Abraham, the volunteers had spent the night of 4th June in their two-man trenches waiting for the attack to come. At the bottom of the trench was a mattress: One slept while the other stood, watched and listened. Abraham's partner was another drummer from Portugal. My father was close-by in another trench.

Within an hour of the commencement of the fierce artillery barrage over the wood, casualties were heavy. The Portuguese next to Abraham was killed by a shell-burst. At some point, somebody called out that Szwarc and Teperman had suffered the same fate.

A short while later, Abraham decided to move out of his trench to seek better shelter from the shell-bursts. Suddenly he slipped into a hole which led into a deep shelter. In the first World War, it had been an ammunitions dump. He spent an hour or two there, in the darkness. After a while he heard a German Soldier, searching the area, shouting *"Raus, Raus!"*

He peered out, raised his hands, and asked for a tree branch to help him get out.

With a few remaining survivors from that wood, he was led off into captivity for the next 5 years.

There were many more facts arising from our meeting, but the essential confirmation of the circumstances of my father's death were now all to clear for me. I thanked Abraham profusely for having helped in my search for the truth.

We left the restaurant and Abraham took me for a walk to his favourite places in Paris. Later we went up to his flat for a coffee and liqueur. He showed me more photographs, particularly taken in Hohenfels, the POW camp. Many prisoners had posed, looking very healthy with their farm and gardening tools and this applied to Schloyme as well. He certainly had put on some weight and was very tanned.

This was not to be my last meeting with former members of the RMVE regiments.

On 21st May 1989, I attended an exceptionally large reunion, organised by the 3 *"Amicales"* in Le Barcares. For a reasonable package price, which covered a hotel room, train, and coach tickets, I joined a big group of volunteers, in Paris. This included wives and, in some cases, their grown-up children. Over the next hours we journeyed by train to Montpelier, where we stayed the night. The following morning, coaches took us on a long bus ride to the *Memoriale* at Le Barcares .

On our arrival we were greeted by the band of the French Foreign Legion and a guard of honour, who presented arms. We all stood to attention for the Marsellaise!

With the assembled flags of the 3 *"Amicales"*, the scene was splendid. There followed innumerable speeches by local dignitaries and the three *"Amicale"* Presidents. General Brothier, who had been a lieutenant in the 22e RMVE recalled the varied origins of the volunteers. Because there had been so many, only a few were integrated into the Legion at the time. The rest were formed into the 3 RMVEs.

The key-note speech was given by General Corre, commanding the Legion. With great praise for the sacrifices given by the regiments in 1940, he recalled the terrible living conditions in Le Barcares in 1939, the uniforms from the wars of 1870 and 1914/18 and the rifles of a similar vintage. He noted that the 22e RMVE had lost 70% of its men. Of the volunteers who were taken captive by the Germans, the Spanish were singled out for harsh treatment. Now stateless, without protection from the Fascist Spanish Government, many perished in concentration camps. Finally, he applauded the adoption of the regiments by the Legion after the war. The ceremony was completed by the unveiling of a new plaque at the entrance to the *Memoriale*, commemorating the 50th anniversary of the creation of the regiments.

We then went to the town hall for a *"Vin d'Honneur"*. After a great number of Kir Royale, we were invited into a restaurant for a sumptuous meal. The wine flowed freely and suddenly there was Vago standing on one of the tables singing his heart out, to the accompaniment of raucous cheers. He was eventually helped down and laid to sleep it off on a bench. A volunteer from Belgium began shouting that the volunteers had been swindled and sold out by France. He was swiftly brought to order by one of the" *Amicale* "Presidents.

Overall, the participants were in high spirits, renewing friendships and sharing memories from the past.

I made many friends that day, particularly among the Jewish volunteers, who welcomed me with open arms. I spoke at length with Ilex Beller, a post-war writer and artist, who recalled the two brothers Szwarc. Some others, recounted to me the loss of their loved ones through deportation, whilst they were prisoners of war. The commitment by the

Vichy Government that the families of those who fought under the French flag would not be arrested, was not respected by the Gestapo.

I was so glad to be part of the celebration and I will recall that day with great pride.

After 3 years, this was a fitting end to my search.

Twenty-three years later, in 1994, I took early retirement from Citroen and, encouraged by my wife and sons, took up academic studies at University College London. Then began, yet another exciting period in my life. I had never imagined that historical research could be so rewarding. After progressing, in the first 6 years, through a couple of degrees on Jewish History and the Holocaust, I embarked on a more ambitious project. It was to research French Government involvement in Illegal immigration to Palestine, in the post-war era.

I felt a close relationship to this period as it coincided with my own time in Paris. Names of politicians such as Georges Bidault, and Ernest Bevin, Foreign ministers of France and the UK, respectively, were objects of hate among my Zionist uncles. French Socialist Ministers, on the other hand, were highly respected, because of their secret efforts on behalf of Jewish refugees.

At the end of a further 6 years, and visits to archives in the UK, France, Israel, and the USA, I finally presented my thesis and was awarded a Doctorate in 2007.

Since then life, for myself and Dot, has been bound up with our sons' marriages and our four grandchildren, the joy of our later life. In June 2018 we celebrated our Golden Wedding.

Alan and Dot with family, Golden Wedding Anniversary

Isaac's army identification bracelet issued to him in September 1939 and returned to the family in November 1941.

The identity bracelet and envelope it was put into after Isaac was reburied in the military cemetery at Villers-Carbonnel, June 1941

Temporary war graves of unidentified soldiers, June1940.

Villers-Carbonnel Military Cemetery. Burial site of some Volunteers of the
22e RMVE, created by French Army in June 1941.

Bois Des Aulnes ,(identified by the arrow). Final location of 9th Company of the 22eRMVE on 5th June 1940.

Concealed entrance to the underground WWI field hospital in the Bois Des Aulnes.

Etienne Vago, the architect of the *"Memoriale"*, October 1988

Le Barcares, "Memoriale des Trois Collones"

Part of the 9th Company of the 22e RMVE at Le Barcares with circled L to R:
Schloyme, Avraham Parizer and Isaac.

Avraham Parizer in his flat, Paris, January 1989.

French Foreign Legion, Guard of Honour before the "Memoriale", Le Barcares. May 1989.

General Corre. Head of the French Foreign Legion at Le Barcares, May 1989.

The Presidents of the three" Amicales" at attention before the *"Memoriale"*.

The band of the French Foreign Legion at Le Barcares

Etienne Vago standing and singing on a table during lunch.

Ilex Beller with former volunteers and relatives during lunch, May 1989.

Freda at Villers-Carbonnel Military Cemetery, May 1992, pointing to a Jewish gravestone.

Photograph of Isaac on the gravestone of the Zelbshilf' organisation, Bagneux, 1992

EPILOGUE

Given the exceptional turn of events, the death of my father and the deportation of Madeleine, Schloyme's wife, I have tried to assess the possible ways my life could have evolved, given different outcomes.

In particular, I have speculated how life would have turned out, if my own father had survived the war or, if he had not, that Schloyme had not lost Madeleine. How with one of those 3 possible outcomes, would my own life have developed, compared to the reality? Would I never have got to appreciate the precious and enduring love of a father?

The first outcome is, of course, the ideal one. I would have lived in Paris with my mother and Isaac, safely returned from the war. More than likely, I would have taken on French Nationality and pursued my education like any other French kid. Ultimately at the age of 18 in 1957, I would have been called up for military service, with the prospect of serving in Algeria, like my cousins Maurice and Loulou had done before me.

In the second outcome, which is the one that prevailed, I would have gained a father in Schloyme, but only for four of my most formative years.

In the third outcome, my mother might have remained a widow in London and I would not have benefited from having a loving father. In that likelihood, I would also have missed the warmth of my French family and the cousins, who are so part of my life now. Above all, my career in finance, which proved so dependent on my knowledge of the French language and culture, could have taken a completely different route.

I believe I was so lucky in many ways, not least that my father's undoubted love for me was replaced by that of another, one who, like my mother, had lost a precious loved one because of the war.

I shall never forget either of them.

APPENDICES

APPENDIX 1

[This is a translation of a unique report which covers the operations of the 9th Company in the few days before my father's death on 5th June 1940.]

"Report by Lieutenant Pierre Dufes, former commander of the 9th company, 22e RMVE to General Frere, former commander of the 7th Army and to General Lenclud, former commander of the 19th Infantry Division.

Date: 1Oth May 1941.

I have the honour to present to you the main operations, between 24th May and 5th June, in which participated the 9th Company of the 22e RMVE, which I had the honour to command.

The 24th may at Fonche-Fonchette, on the road to Perrone, after a night march of 40 kms, order to attack at 8am.

The 9th deploys on a front of 1,500 metres, to the east of the Route Nationale, in staggered lines, because it has to keep to the right. Contact is made at Licourt which is reoccupied without difficulty. Resistance is reported between Licourt and Misery, which one must reach, without fail. On the outskirts of Licourt, severe artillery barrage, shells and a few 105's.

We advance beyond the barrage and the outskirts of Misery are reached. The barrage continues on Licourt, where the enemy obviously believes we have retreated. Search and evacuation of the wounded.

Second Lieutenant Tiedrez (1st Section) progressing through the woods captures 6 prisoners. Acting Capitain Guitard (4th Section) who, at my side, experienced being under fire for the first time, proved to be very energetic. He drew his pistol to force a few volunteers, who appeared to hesitate to obey orders to advance.

I try to establish contact with the Battalion.

A courier of the Battalion brings me the order to occupy Misery, to stop the advance and to resist on the spot at all costs, protecting myself on all sides. The 2nd Battalion had suffered severe losses and was retreating to Fresne-Mazencourt to regroup.

The Company installs itself in Misery, as the enemy breaks contact without difficulty, leaving equipment, munitions and even food snacks. Moral is excellent.

We place ourselves in the central junction of Misery where every exit is barricaded. Double sentries at exits. During the night, a few rifle shots. I establish contact with the Battalion.

The following day, situation is stabilised to our left. Battalion HQ establishes itself in Misery. 9th Company receive orders to move to the farm 800m N.E of the Chateau Parc and hide in the hedgerows. Severe artillery barrage during advance. A few losses. I install my command post in the farmhouse. Physical activity and patrol contact with the 41st Infantry Regiment, heavily engaged towards St.Christ .A fairly disorganised battalion from this regiment retreats to our right. Orders to resist on the spot. But no attack. Next day the battalion of the 41st, now regrouped, brilliantly retakes its positions.

We change position many times in the sector. We advance, notably into the woods, in close in liaison with the 10th Company, in preparation for an attack, which is abandoned. A few artillery barrages without major damage. One night a soldier is wounded during a skirmish.

Orders to relieve the Ist Company of the Regiment which has been under continuous fire in the woods facing Horgny, west of the Route Nationale. We are replaced by a company from the 112th Infantry Regiment. Our Battalion Chief, Commander Aussy, is evacuated, seriously ill. Capitaine De Franclieu who commanded the 10th, takes command of the Battalion.. He comes to inspect my positions and establishes a phone contact with Battalion HQ. We reorganise the position previously held by the 1st Company. We are an arrows flight from Horgny and Villers-Carbonnel.. Behind us is the 2nd Battalion. Mine laying by the engineering corps over 2 nights. We are very exposed and shelled on this occasion. It is foreseen that we will soon launch an attack.

Here, I suffer a very painful incident. Whilst moving during the night through the woods, I am blinded by a branch and suffer a lot. (Witnesses: Capitaine de Franclieu and, commanding the Battalion, Capitaine Leenhardt, commander of the 2nd Company, who is further back on my left). I am treated on the spot at my command post by the assistant doctor Joel, very attentive.

4th June, noise of vehicles moving opposite. Sergeant Solny (2nd Section) volunteers to carry out a patrol up to the Horgny farm. He reports that it is unoccupied at the beginning of night. I telephone the Battalion and speak to Sergeant-Major Milhet. Soon our artillery opens fire to the rear of Villers-Carbonnel. Everything seems calm when, after midnight, a note from the Battalion warns me of an imminent German attack. First shells towards 3 am and then intense shelling of my positions, which causes us losses. [My father is killed at this moment] Order received to resist on the spot and to hold on. A number of German soldiers near Horgny farm and a massive launch of a [German] attack in tight formations. Immediate Counter-fire by our artillery. Our heavy machine gun, in a group commanded by corporal Coquart at 15 metres to the left of my command post, pinpoints the small ravine coming out of Horgny and works wonders. Also very efficient fire from our lighter machine guns (F.Ms) Bullets fly back to us but the enemy keeps a low profile.

At times, heavy smoke. I launch two rockets, only to receive an artillery barrage. I order the 60mm mortar, hidden 30meters to the rear of my command post, hidden in a large haystack, to fire on the slopes of Horgny. Planes fly at low level over the woods where I am located, but without dropping bombs.

After their passage, we note flames licking up from the ground (Incendiary grenades?). I am encircled once by them but without harm. Adjudant Poirson, chief of my Command Section, is injured. The attack appears to have been discontinued. The shelling recommences intensely. I move to the north east exit from the wood to observe what is happening on the Route National on my right. Standing facing the road, I catch a violent blow to my kidneys (a piece of shrapnel which lodges deeply). I return in pain to my command post. Unable to staunch the flow of blood, and being in a fairly bad state, I decide to have myself tended to. I pass command to Second-lieutenant Tiedrez. He soon lost both legs through a shell burst at the same time as Acting Officer Guitard is injured to his knee and hip.

Losses were very heavy. Today, particularly for the volunteers, numbers can only be measured approximately. All 3 Officers unfit for duty on the morning of 5th June

Non-commissioned officers: All 11 either injured, killed or captured.

Volunteers: Only 140 men on 5th June as a result of past losses. When I arrived at the command post of the 2nd Battalion at Fresne-Mazencourt, I saw many injured, belonging mainly to the 4th and 2nd Sections of my Company.

Acting officer Guitard (4th Section) reported to me that at the time he was injured, the Company numbered but 40 uninjured soldiers. On 25th June, a volunteer from the 9th Company; Josef Ocio was present at the RMVE depot at Septfond. He had been captured on 6th June but had immediately escaped.

I have the honour to recommend for a merit award the following:

2 officers, 4 non-commissioned officers, I corporal, I volunteer.

I attach to this report a list of recommendations linked to the Sections which I personally commanded, without the list being complete, in view of the circumstances.

In support of this report, I refer to:

The Journal de Marche, presented by Commander Hermann, Commander of the Regiment.

My battalion Commander Capitaine de Franclieu who, injured on 6th June, escaped and is presently at the 23rd R.I. in Toulouse

For a specific deed, mentioned in the Report, carried out by Capitaine Leenhardt, commander of the 2nd Battalion of the regiment, injured, who last September was being treated at the Montpelier Hospital.

Signed: Pierre Dufes

67 Quai Pierre Seize, Lyon"

APPENDIX 2

Map (a) showing location of Bois des Aulnes.

APPENDIX 3

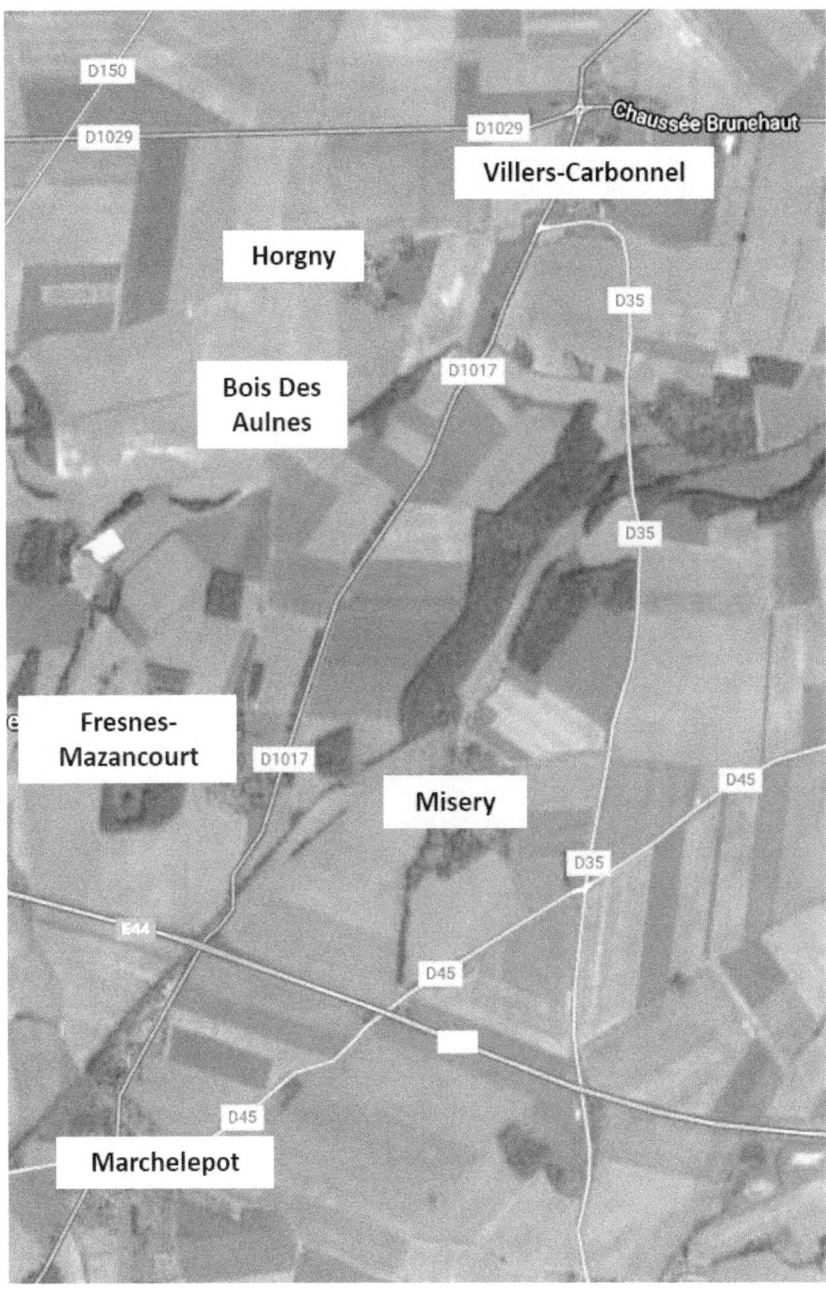

Map (b) Bois des Aulnes and villages at centre of battle.

APPENDIX 4

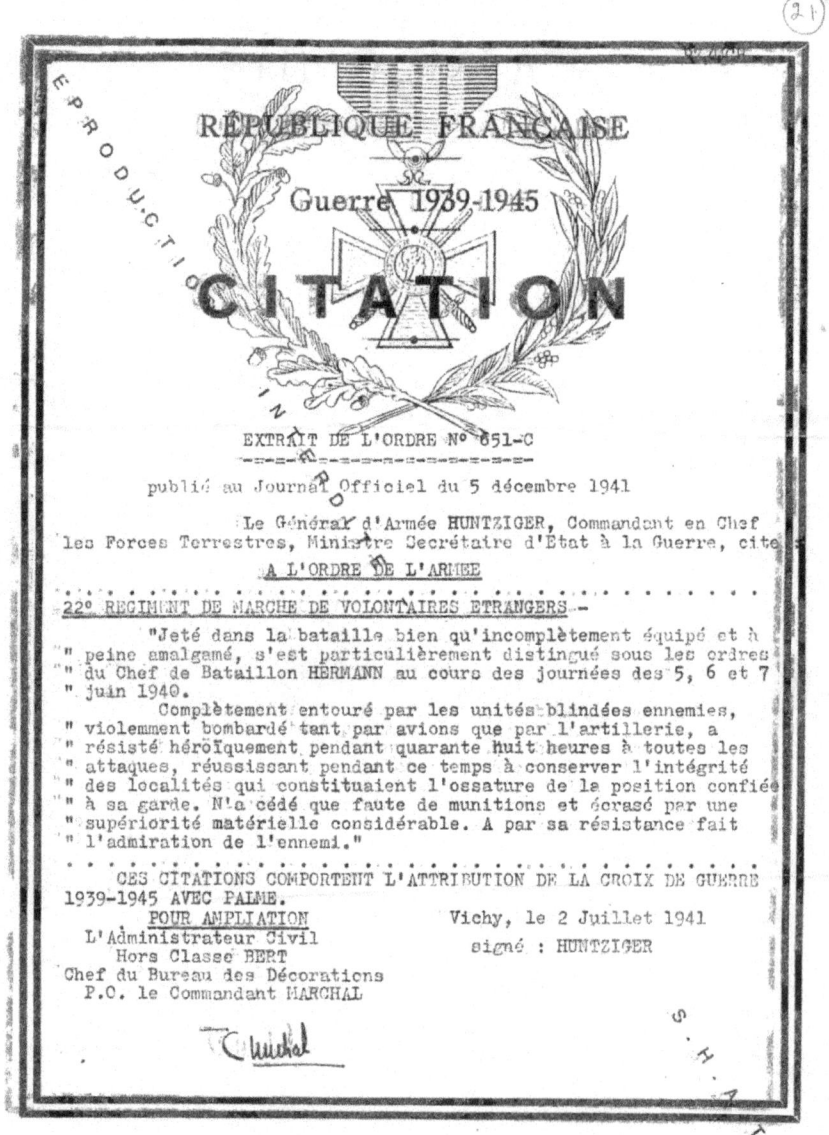

RÉPUBLIQUE FRANÇAISE

Guerre 1939-1945

CITATION

EXTRAIT DE L'ORDRE N° 651-C

publié au Journal Officiel du 5 décembre 1941

Le Général d'Armée HUNTZIGER, Commandant en Chef les Forces Terrestres, Ministre Secrétaire d'Etat à la Guerre, cite

A L'ORDRE DE L'ARMEE

22° REGIMENT DE MARCHE DE VOLONTAIRES ETRANGERS.-

"Jeté dans la bataille bien qu'incomplètement équipé et à peine amalgamé, s'est particulièrement distingué sous les ordres du Chef de Bataillon HERMANN au cours des journées des 5, 6 et 7 juin 1940.
Complètement entouré par les unités blindées ennemies, violemment bombardé tant par avions que par l'artillerie, a résisté héroïquement pendant quarante huit heures à toutes les attaques, réussissant pendant ce temps à conserver l'intégrité des localités qui constituaient l'ossature de la position confiée à sa garde. N'a cédé que faute de munitions et écrasé par une supériorité matérielle considérable. A par sa résistance fait l'admiration de l'ennemi."

CES CITATIONS COMPORTENT L'ATTRIBUTION DE LA CROIX DE GUERRE 1939-1945 AVEC PALME.

POUR AMPLIATION
L'Administrateur Civil
Hors Classe BERT
Chef du Bureau des Décorations
P.O. le Commandant MARCHAL

Vichy, le 2 Juillet 1941
signé : HUNTZIGER

Citation of the French Army and Croix De Guerre awarded to 22 RMVE in July 1941

APPENDIX 5

TRANSCRIPTION.- L'an mil neuf cent quarante, le six
Juin, est décédé "MORT POUR LA FRANCE", à Villers Car-
-bonnel (Somme) SZWarC Icchok Ajryk, soldat du 22ème
régiment de marche de volontaires étrangers, inscrit
au recrutement de CENTRAL REUILLY sous le n° 9683, né
le sept octobre mil neuf cent-sept à Wlcolawek (Polo-
-gne) domicilié en dernier lieu 13, rue des Immeubles
Industriels à PARIS, XI°, fils de Abraham et de Reche-
-la, époux de FURST Fréda. Le présent acte a été dres-
-sé par Nous.- Transcrit le dix juillet mil neuf cent
quarante-quatre, neuf heures cinquante, par Nous.-

Pour Extrait conforme,
Paris, le premier Avril mil neuf cent cinquante-sept.

Le Maire-Adjoint.

Isaac Szwarc's death certificate issued by the town hall of the 11th District of
Paris.

147

Part translation:

"6th June 1940 deceased " Mort pour La France" at Villers-Carbonnel
(Somme) Szwarc , Icchok, Ajryk, soldier of the 22nd Infantry Regiment of
Foreign Volunteers, registered at Central Reuilly under number 9683,
born 7th October 1907 in Wloklawek,(Poland). Last known address: 13
rue des Immeubles Industrielles, Paris 11e, son of Abraham and Rechela,
husband of Freda Furst........"

Lightning Source UK Ltd.
Milton Keynes UK
UKHW041137191020
371842UK00001B/279

9 781800 316416